Dawn of a Millennium

Also by Erich Harth

Windows on the Mind

Dawn of a Millennium

BEYOND EVOLUTION AND CULTURE

Erich Harth

Little, Brown & Company
Boston · Toronto · London

Library of Congress Cataloging-in-Publication Data

Harth, Erich.
Dawn of a millennium: beyond evolution and culture / by Erich Harth. — 1st ed.
    p.   cm.
  Bibliography: p.
  Includes index.
  ISBN 0-316-34851-1
  1. Brain — Evolution.   2. Human evolution.   3. Neurobiology-Philosophy.
I. Title.
QP376.H292   1990
612.8′2′01 — dc20   89-12462
                                    CIP

10 9 8 7 6 5 4 3 2 1

FG

Published simultaneously in Canada
by Little, Brown & Company (Canada) Limited

PRINTED IN THE UNITED STATES OF AMERICA

For S. H.
in loving memory

Acknowledgments

This is to thank my wife, Dorothy, and my sons, Peter and Rick, for their encouragement and many spirited discussions. They have provided me with a steady stream of ideas, sources, and events that have been woven into this book. I owe much, also, to my editor, Roger Donald, for his dedication to this project and his penetrating critique.

Contents

Dawn of a Millennium

Introduction

In the Pacific Ocean off the Galapagos Islands, at a depth of some eight thousand feet, the ocean bottom is torn deep down to its infrastructure. Hot gases and chemicals stream out continuously from these *thermal vents,* making the surrounding waters lethal to all but a select group of organisms, crustaceans mostly, but also some vertebrates that are uniquely adapted to this strange environment. Scientists have become familiar with the giant clams and the bizarre-looking six-foot-long tube worms that populate this world in great numbers.

Recently a fish belonging to a previously unknown species of the genus *Bythites* was discovered there. As it was pulled up from its cozy world, it gave birth to live young and then died, together with its multitude of offspring, before reaching the sunlit world of the waiting scientists.

The physiology of these creatures is different from that of other life-forms. Without sunlight, they are dependent on chemosynthesis for their energy source. They cannot venture far from the vicinity of the hot, mineral-rich environment of the hydrothermal vents. Their world ends where the temperature drops and the mineral concentration is diluted by the ordinary cold water of the ocean floor.

But the vents are ephemeral. Scientists estimate that a particular crack may have a lifetime of only one or two decades. Shifting of the suboceanic strata causes active vents to close and new vents to open somewhere else. The closing of a vent must mean the end of life for the microworld that enjoyed its warmth and mineral riches. How it is possible for some survivors to reach new, similar, worlds, and thus perpetuate the species, is still a mystery. But this evidently happens, because these life-forms could not possibly evolve in the brief lifespan of an individual hydrothermal vent.

The planet Earth is unique among all the bodies in our solar system. The chemistry of its atmosphere and surface and its precise place in the field of radiation of the sun are just right for the rich variety in its plant and animal kingdoms and its dominant species, *Homo sapiens.* Apart from a few ups and downs — there is some evidence that periodic cataclysmic events have occurred every thirty million years or so — conditions on earth have been relatively stable and favorable to our kind of life for several billion years.

Clearly this situation will not last forever. Our sun is an ordinary star with a predictable future. It will evolve along a known trajectory, at the end of which it will die. This will not happen for a few billion years, and it is hoped that mankind,[1] if it is still around then, in whatever form, will have found the means to leave this dying "vent" to find the warmth and light of another sun. Perhaps by then we will have spread out to populate the galaxy.

In this event we will have gained considerable lease on life. But it appears now that the universe as a whole had a definite beginning and may come to a dramatic end. The present expansion may be followed by an accelerating collapse — stars and galaxies moving ever closer into each other's gravitational grasp, the whole thing ending with a final apocalyptic crunch. There can be no survival.

Freeman Dyson, a contemporary theoretical physicist, contemplates this eventuality:

> There is great melancholy in the picture of a finite universe, its life force spent, its days of passion over, counting the hours remaining before it slides into oblivion. What will our last poets sing, whoever they may be, human or alien, as they watch the stars crowding together and streaming faster and faster across the imploding sky?[2]

It is also possible that the opposite will happen: the universe may continue to expand forever. In the infinitely thinned-out space no new stars will be born, and the old ones will eventually have spent their nuclear fuels and turned into lifeless cinders or black holes.

But Dyson is more optimistic about this scenario. He envisions new life-forms adapting to virtually empty space and temperatures near absolute zero. He speaks convincingly of the possibility of intelligent organisms with truly cosmic dimensions, taking in the incredibly diffuse radiative energy from very distant sources. In the eternally expanding universe he conceives of life continuing forever, but life that would be very different from anything living today.

Dyson's visions are brave, awe-inspiring, and controversial. Our minds boggle at the thought of descendants billions of years hence that may have less resemblance to us than we have to protozoans. It is difficult to have empathy with those creatures of a distant and questionable future, whose bodies may span as much space as is now occupied by a galaxy.

In the meanwhile, as the end of the twentieth century approaches, man is an endangered and puzzled primate. Our problems are menacing. Unlike the bythites and the tube worms, our genes are poorly adapted to our present physical environment and to our life-style, since our last significant genetic changes occurred several hundred thousand years ago, when humans roamed a very different earth in scattered bands of hunter-gatherers. Evolution left us stranded in the African savannah at the dawn of human civilization.

Our genetic obsolescence is apparent in the foods we crave. We like fats, sugars, and salt, all of which we generally consume in quantities that are detrimental to our health. Our tastes — it was pointed out by Melvin Konner — are likely to be genetic, acquired during long periods of evolutionary history during which these three vital ingredients were in scarce supply.[3] Physical exertion was a daily routine for primitive humans, and in times of hardship even a small reserve of body fat could have made the difference between starvation and survival. Adaptive mutations, such as our appetites, are not easily reversed by evolution, which cares little whether we die of heart disease after reaching middle age.

If *nature,* by way of our genes, supplies us with the wrong signals, the lessons we receive from our civilization, generally referred to as *nurture,* have often steered us into calamitous situations.

It was the appearance among hominids of a superior brain that gave rise to the beginnings of a civilization and perhaps marked the end of natural selection. Adaptation through the inherently slow genetic changes became an outmoded process. Instead man began to use a faculty that was new in the ecological equation: he had acquired a *mind.* He became the first organism able to observe himself, judge his own actions, to project into past and future, and to act at times in ways that conflicted with both his biological drives and his culturally acquired values. He adapted to his changing needs, not by waiting for favorable mutations, but by building shelters, making fires, inventing tools. Conscious of his unequalled intelligence, he has given himself the epithet *sapiens sapiens,* the doubly wise.

But, evidently not wise enough. Mind, which has propelled us from the Stone Age to our present technological peak in just a few millennia, is still falling victim to some age-old genes. Our ready anger and combative temperament, which may have been useful in the hunter-gatherer's competition for food, had lost its adaptive advantage long before in the era of push-button nuclear weaponry. And yet, the present century has been an infamous chapter in our history. Two devastating world wars and numerous minor ones have left us with untold millions killed and maimed, cities incinerated, and precious resources wantonly spent on destruction. The atrocities committed in this century against defenseless civilian populations — often with state approval and instigation — rival in scope and brutality the worst we have seen in the last two thousand years. This, too, is occasion for "great melancholy."

Through it all, we have clung to the notion that none of this would have happened had it not been for mankind's eternal division into the good and the evil, the righteous and the guilty, the considerate and the irresponsible, those of the right and those of the wrong faith, the trustworthy and the perfidious. The amount of self-deception required to maintain faith in this myth does not do honor to our thinking processes.

We are slow to acknowledge the profound changes (mostly man-made) our environment has undergone. I want to examine here not so much the technical problems raised by the threats of nuclear annihilation, overpopulation, and pollution, as our own willingness and *resolve* to do what intelligence tells us we must do in order to survive. This is more a psychological and cultural problem than a scientific one. Our ability to make the right choices will depend less on technological know-how than on our readiness to overcome prejudice, greed, lethargy, and the comfortable notion that things can't be all that urgent because mankind has been facing similar problems for a long time. We tend to think of ourselves as moving along a timeline of virtually endless progression, a kind of *historical relativity*. We like to interpret anything new as just another form of past events, a perpetual *déjà vu*. We convince ourselves that "there is nothing new under the sun," and conclude that we can go on indefinitely without major change in our strategies.

Nothing could be farther from the truth. It is safe to say that, with the triple threats of population explosion, environmental decay, and annihilation by nuclear conflict, we have entered a stage of acute instability that makes short-range survival (decades to a few centuries) questionable and a long-range future almost improbable.

The arrival of a new year is always an occasion for a brief look into the past and some passing resolutions. It is an artificial and symbolic hiatus in the flow of time. New decades seem particularly significant, centuries even more so. I remember being told, as a child, of the delirious and frenetic celebrations greeting the year 1900, the beginning of the twentieth century. We can expect an unprecedented amount of merriment, soul-searching, and prognostication when the three terminal zeroes pass in review. By coincidence, mankind will be passing through a critical threshold at about that time. We are beginning to appreciate that the real dangers facing humanity in the coming decades are not from some intractable subgroup of the human race but from global problems affecting all of us equally. The dangers have been described with increasing frequency and urgency, but actions are slow to follow in the wake of recognition. There is also the risk of overexposure: unpleasant truths are likely to become formalized into a kind of litany, making our concerns ceremonial rather than an active part of our lives. A French philosopher once said that "if you don't do what reason tells you to do, you don't think enough." And Nietzsche said:

> In the whirlpool of forces man stands with the conceit that this whirlpool is rational and has a rational aim: an error! The only rational thing we know is what little reason man has: he must exert it a lot, and it is always ruinous for him when he abandons himself to "Providence."[4]

To think is to project. Only the human mind is capable of folding together past and future in order to direct our present actions, overriding where necessary both instinct and convention, in what I will call the *creative loop.*

The writing of this book has been my own subjective way of assessing our intellectual and emotional readiness to face the challenges. I have assembled in these pages a retrospective and perspective that are entirely my own and leave it to the reader to make the resolutions. My perspective is that of the twentieth century. Born soon after World War I, I may perhaps catch a glimpse of the new millennium. But it is not my age. My sons' lives will bridge the two epochs. It is for them and their contemporaries that I have undertaken this effort. I see the coming era as a time when the rational mind must finally assert itself against the pull of our old genes and the lure of our old ways. History, it has been said, is the friend of war. It has also been the ally of mindless abuse inflicted on our habitat and on the creatures with whom we are sharing it. Our future cannot tolerate more such history.

CHAPTER I

Time, Rhythms, and the Millennium

THE PASSAGE OF TIME has always been an irritant we try to assuage by looking for cyclic repetitions, for *rhythms* to give us a sense of familiarity and the illusion of security. Heraclitus, perhaps to dispel that illusion, perhaps merely in wonder at the greatest puzzle in nature, which is physical change, remarked that "you cannot step into the same river twice." Time forms no loops. No moment ever returns.

It is a paradox that the instruments with which we keep track of time virtually never change. The pendulum keeps returning to the same spot, the quartz oscillator in your watch repeats cycle after cycle as though there were no time. Perhaps this timelessness, this incorruptibility, is the reason we feel so comfortable with cycles.

Alexander Marshak, an archaeologist at the Peabody Museum of Harvard University, has studied some of the earliest forms of record keeping, predating written language by some twenty-five thousand years.[1] He describes one artifact, a flat, oval piece of bone on which thirty thousand years ago someone had incised a series of markings that snake back and forth, "turning as the ox ploughs." He interprets their meaning as the record of some recurring event, perhaps the phases of the moon. We can only guess what comfort the Ice Age human derived from these rhythmic recurrences.

A full moon may reappear in a different setting, under different circumstances, and yet with a reassuring sameness. It is not an older moon, and when spring comes around next time it is not an older spring. Whether the timepiece is a pendulum, the sun, or the moon, time is measured through endless repetition. Many such unchanging rhythms keep pace with our ebbing lives.

Cycles seem reassuring for other reasons. We feel that in a world in which conditions change without the restraint of cycles, things will get out of hand. The appearance of a comet seems to upset the comforting regularity in the sky, which is probably why it used to be taken as a harbinger of misfortunes. Eventually we learned that comets, too, are part of the Newtonian clockwork of the heavens.

In a brave bit of optimism the Babylonians, and centuries later, Plato, believed in a grand cycle of 36,000 years, the *Great Year,* in which *everything* is repeated.[2]

Nonrepetitive changes conjure up the specter of changes without limit, or with catastrophic limits, like a population explosion, or a spreading epidemic. At best, the future seems uncertain, clouded by the threat of unprecedented disasters. The *apocalyptic* view stems from this feeling that in a nonrepetitive setting, conditions just cannot for long remain favorable to human life.

The fear of Armageddon was very real in the Middle Ages. "The stupendous drama of the Last Days," writes Norman Cohn, "was not a fantasy about some remote and indefinite future, but a prophesy which was infallible, and which at almost any given moment was felt to be at the point of fulfilment."[3]

With cycles we know what we are in for, and if things are now getting worse, we know they must get better eventually. Springs follow the bitterest winters, and there is nothing so bad that we haven't already experienced and withstood it.

The cycles we deal with come in all sizes. To the short ones, like our own heartbeat and breathing, we pay little attention. Even the intervals measured out by the daily rising and setting of the sun are short enough for us to note no change from one day to the next. Sleep may not rejuvenate us, but it restores us, or almost restores us to the point we left twenty-four hours earlier. But years, and their multiples, are another matter. We lie at anniversaries and reunions when we tell each other that we "haven't changed a bit."

Then there are the big cycles that transcend our own life span and whose comings and goings we observe only on rare occasions: the return of Halley's comet, the turning of a century or a millennium.

But what about the long trends, especially as they affect life on earth? Before Darwin, it was the accepted view that, once created by divine act, the universe and the life-forms contained in it were essentially in a *steady state*.[4] Each species of the flora and fauna was created in its final form, to coexist with all the others in a delicate equilibrium. This is precarious enough, as I have pointed out, but not as disquieting as evolution, which takes us progressively toward an unknown future.

Approaching A.D. 1000

"A thousand years" has the ring of a timespan of almost transhistoric proportions. Hitler promised longevity of a thousand years for his Third Reich. In the early interpretation of the New Testament the millennium was to be the end of history as it was known, the apocalypse.

The year A.D. 1000 was preceded by many predictions of doom, but mankind has survived it, and we are now rapidly approaching A.D. 2000. We have little reason for complacency, however. Religious and ideological intolerance and ethnic strife are threatening our civilization now to an even greater degree than a thousand years ago, and nuclear devastation is an ever-present threat. Religious fatalism paralyzed thought in the Dark Ages; we now often fall prey to scientific fatalism: the feeling that human survival into the twenty-first century is doubtful, given the fundamental instability of the nuclear standoff.

We begin our look into the future with a glance at the past. The choice of the year A.D. 1000 as the target of our reminiscing is a reflection of our preoccupation with cycles and anniversaries. Indeed, there is no reason to suspect that anything in human affairs should be repeated with any kind of regularity, let alone in neat intervals of a thousand years. But, sentimentalists that we are, we will soon celebrate the completion of another thousand travels around the sun. It seems not inappropriate, therefore, to recall the last time that happened.

But there is more than sentimentality to our backward look. Social historians still debate the issue of whether history teaches us anything. I believe it does. Even though true repetitions, as Heraclitus taught us, are nonexistent, there are trends and threads that show remarkable persistence. We see mankind confronted throughout history by very similar problems, in particular territorial and ideological conflicts and all kinds of tribal hostilities. It is almost impossible for most of us to divorce ourselves from the prejudices of our own group. And so we view the present through a veil of bias and partisanship. Our likes and aversions also have long histories, which makes us participants rather than spectators even in events that happened long ago. The value of this backward look lies, I believe, in our ability to perceive contemporary problems in unfamiliar settings, and thus less encumbered with emotional baggage. We may have to go back a thousand years to gain a measure of detachment.

The Middle Ages stretched from the fall of the Roman Empire to Columbus. The tenth century, often called the darkest of the Dark Ages, the "nadir of human intellect," lay at its very center. But "if it was dark," Lynn White tells us, "its darkness was that of the womb."[5] It was, in fact, a period of gestation.

In the early tenth century Europe was a vast and desolate place, with clusters of people thinly scattered in lamentable circumstances. The Carolingian Empire was nearing its end, and Rome, still calling itself the capital of the world, a "toothless harlot." Almost daily bands of marauders — Vikings, Arabs, and Magyars — threatened the lives of people in towns and the countryside. The raids were generally brief and devastating and rarely involved ideological or territorial ambitions.

But all was not bleak. The famous Medical School of Salerno was said to have been founded about the year 900 by a Jew, an Arab, a Greek, and a Latin. It was to become the place where Hellenistic and Arab medical science were first introduced into Europe. In Venice St. Mark's cathedral was nearing completion, only to be destroyed by fire later that century. But a campanile constructed in 902 was to last exactly 1000 years. It collapsed in 1902.

A semblance of order existed in Spain, where the Omayad dynasty flowered until about the end of the tenth century, and where

Christians, Jews, and Arab Muslims coexisted in relative peace. Meanwhile, to the East, the Byzantine Empire was still expanding, but was finding itself more and more threatened by the surrounding Muslim world.

The status of European Jews, while precarious, was not yet desperate. They existed in loosely scattered communities and, because of their learning and contact with diverse cultures, were often entrusted with delicate diplomatic missions.

Long-distance trade was carried on despite the uncertain times, especially by some of the Italian coastal cities. Venice, in particular, was engaged in commerce with both Christian Byzantium and its Arab neighbors. At one point the Byzantine emperor demanded a strict embargo on war materials sold to the "Saracens." It was to be understood that

> from now on no one is to be so bold as to carry weapons for sale or for gift to Saracen territory, nor lumber for building ships that may cause damage to the Christian people, nor breastplates, nor shields, nor swords, nor lances, nor other weapons with which the Saracens may strike Christians; but one may only carry weapons with which one may defend oneself from enemies, and these cannot in any way be sold or given to the barbarians. As for lumber we concede that we are not to carry elms, maples, broad planks, oars, spars, or other lumber that may cause harm to Christians, but we may carry only trimmed logs of ash five feet long and one ax wide, and vases, bowls and cups, and tree planks likewise five or six feet long.[6]

We are suddenly propelled into our own time again. Translate the items into their modern equivalents, and we find many startling parallels. The distinction between civilian goods and potential war materials has a particularly contemporary ring.

As the Byzantine Empire weakened, the Islamic states, from the Cordovan Caliphate in Spain across North Africa and eastward as far as Bukhara and Samarkand in Central Asia, developed a rich culture of their own. It was here that Greek heritage was fused with Oriental culture, a mixture that was later to become the raw material for the Renaissance.

A number of important developments took place as the tenth century drew to a close. Northern Europe became Christianized, borders began to stabilize, the raids by Norsemen and Magyars declined in frequency, and the map of modern Europe began to emerge. In the East, the Poles declared their allegiance to the Pope, and the Bulgars, once the scourge of the Balkans, were brutally subdued and subsequently Christianized. The Russians were luckier: they joined the fold when Vladimir of Kiev became a convert to Christianity and married Princess Anne, the daughter of the Byzantine emperor.

At the same time the hostility between the Christian and Muslim world increased sharply. In 994 Arabs destroyed the monastery of Monte Cassino, near Naples, and by the end of the century a fierce economic competition had developed between the territories defined by the two faiths.

Two widely separated but significant events are often cited as having occurred close to the year 1000: one was the invention of gunpowder in China, the other the probable discovery of America. German and Danish chronicles of the time report the Danes coming upon an island they called Vinland the Good because "vines grow without cultivation, producing the best wine . . . in addition, crops abound there even without planting . . ."[7]

Spark in the Summer Forest

While the widespread fears of Armageddon and the Last Judgment, predicted for the year 1000, did not materialize, the new millennium brought neither increased tranquility nor understanding. On the contrary, religious fervor and intolerance deepened, and most conflicts were now strictly along religious and ethnic lines. In 1002 Pope Sylvester II sent an expeditionary force south in an abortive attempt to take Jerusalem from the "Infidels." Nine years later al Hakim, the "mad caliph" of the Fatimid Empire, destroyed the Church of the Holy Sepulcher in Jerusalem. Still, the last reservoir of goodwill was not yet completely exhausted. Muslims helped to rebuild the church a few years later. It appears that non-Muslim faiths were still mostly respected after that, and that Christian pilgrims were given free access to their holy places.

The world of human faiths was further fragmented when Pope Leo IX characterized the Patriarchy of Constantinople as "an assembly of heretics" and "a synagogue of Satan." Soon thereafter, in 1054, the two churches were permanently and irreconcilably split, in what came to be known as the Great Schism.

The comparative peace that existed in Jerusalem after al Hakim the Mad ended dramatically when the Turks took Jerusalem from the Fatimids in 1070. Stories of desecrations and attacks upon Christians became frequent then. Xenophobia intensified on both sides of the issue. The fateful step was taken by Pope Urban II. On a cold November day in 1095 he made an emotional appeal to a large audience in the Auvergne. It was called by Will Durant "the most influential speech in medieval history."

> O race of Franks! race beloved and chosen by God! . . . From the confines of Jerusalem and from Constantinople a grievous report has gone forth that an accursed race, wholly alienated from God, has violently invaded the lands of these Christians, and has depopulated them by pillage and fire. They have led away a part of the captives into their own country, and a part they have killed by cruel tortures. They destroy the altars, after having defiled them with their uncleanliness. . . .
>
> On whom, then rests the labor of avenging these wrongs, and of recovering this territory, if not upon you — you upon whom, above all others, God has conferred remarkable glory in arms, great bravery, and strength to humble the heads of those who resist you? Let the deeds of your ancestors encourage you — the glory and grandeur of Charlemagne and your other monarchs. Let the Holy Sepulcher of Our Lord and Saviour, now held by unclean nations, arouse you, and the holy places that are now stained with pollution. . . . Let none of your possessions keep you back, nor anxiety for your family affairs. For this land which you now inhabit, shut in on all sides by the sea and the mountain peaks, is too narrow for your large population; it scarcely furnishes food enough for its cultivators. Hence it is that you murder and devour one another, that you wage wars, and that many among you perish in civil strife.
>
> Let hatred, therefore, depart from among you; let your quarrels end. Enter upon the road to the Holy Sepulcher; wrest that land from a wicked race, and subject it to yourselves. Jerusalem is a land fruitful above all others, a paradise of delights. That royal city, situated at the center of the

earth, implores you to come to her aid. Undertake this journey eagerly for the remission of your sins, and be assured of the reward of imperishable glory in the Kingdom of Heaven.[8]

It was not lost on the crowd that the call to "glory and grandeur" also held out the promise of a "paradise of delights" and perhaps of escape from their dismal economic plight. At any rate, the response was immediate and enthusiastic. According to Robert the Monk, who has given us the above version of Urban's speech, "all who were present . . . cried out 'It is the will of God! It is the will of God!'" And so the Holy Crusades were launched on that day. They were to last for two hundred years.

Urban's appeal, and its ready echo in the sentiment of the masses, merits some analysis. There is a thought-provoking timelessness in its demagoguery, which pretends to address the highest, but succeeds in rousing the lowest, instincts. Note the recital of atrocities calling for righteous outrage; the depiction of the adversary as subhuman, "unclean," and "alienated from God"; the appeal to honor, pride; the call for unity within, for brotherhood to face the enemy outside, forsaking family and worldly goods; and, finally, the promise of both earthly and heavenly rewards.

Harvest of Hate

From the open field in Clermont in the Auvergne, Urban's call spread quickly across Europe from England to Italy. But the most zealous response came from northeastern France and western Germany, regions impoverished by years of droughts and floods and terrorized by plagues. Here the desperate poor eagerly listened to itinerant "prophets" like Peter the Hermit, who called for a pilgrimage in arms. Incited by a mixture of penitential fervor and compensatory fantasies of riches and glory, an ill-equipped rabble of the poor was joined by renegade monks, robbers, and brigands. This beggar's army, the dreaded *Tafurs*, in the wake of their push south, left a trail of plundered villages and towns, in which many of the inhabitants had been raped and murdered.[9]

But the pretense of high purpose, the fulfillment of "the will of God," was never lost. The Crusade was hailed by contemporaries as the greatest event in the history of mankind.

The Jews of Europe, who in the tenth century had experienced a high degree of prosperity, peace, and recognition, were among the first to suffer at the hands of the mobs. Accusing them of sending warnings of the gathering Crusade to the Arabs, the Crusaders turned on many Jewish communities, killing, raping, and plundering. Thousands lost their lives here in the first large-scale massacres of European Jews.

As they passed through the Balkans and Greece, the intense xenophobia of the central Europeans caused them to treat the Byzantine Christians, Copts, and Christian Arabs with arrogance, contempt, and often the same violence they had exercised against the Jews. The excesses of the mob were rarely kept in check by the commanders of the venture. Indeed, they were considered to be an inevitable part of the noble purpose and included in the will of God. When a force of Crusaders approached the gates of Caesarea, a prosperous city in Palestine, two Muslims implored the invaders to spare the lives of the citizens. "Lords, you who are masters and doctors of the Christian law, why do you command your people to kill us, to invade our country, when it is written in your religion that no one must kill anyone who is in the image of your God, or carry off his goods?" they asked. The answer was that "he who fights to destroy the law of God must be killed in just vengeance. . . . We ask you to give up the land of St. Peter, and we will let you go safe and sound, your persons and your goods. If you will not do so, the Lord will kill you with his sword. . . ."[10]

The Crusaders finally reached their goal, and Jerusalem was captured. The reports of what happened there are among the most graphic descriptions of human savagery. They must be believed, since the chroniclers, many of them clerics, accompanied the Crusaders. Some 70,000 Muslims were slaughtered, many after being tortured for days. Yet there was hardly any note of condemnation of these excesses. The carnage was just. The Infidels deserved their fate, and it pleased God that these acts were carried out. The Jews of the city fared no better than their Muslim brethren; they were herded into the main synagogue and burned alive.

A few of the Muslims had survived on the roof of a mosque, after being promised their lives by the Norman leader Tancred in exchange for a heavy ransom. But soldiers scaled the wall and beheaded every man and woman "save those who threw themselves off the roof to their death."[11] Having finished, the victorious Christians gathered in the Church of the Holy Sepulcher, and "embracing one another, they wept with joy and release, and thanked the God of Mercies for their victory."[12]

Stampede into the Future

We cannot read these reports without profound shock. Is this because we fail to recognize ourselves, or because we recognize ourselves too well? The inhumanity — we call it that because we pretend such actions are those of other species, not ours — seems to belong to a particularly dark chapter of our history, with the characters seen as in a wax museum, no longer part of our real world. The atrocities of our own epoch appear somehow in a different light. We piously believe that Bergen-Belsen, MyLai, Sabra, and Shattila are aberrations, much less characteristic of *our* nature than the rape of Jerusalem was of people in the Dark Ages.

We may speculate whether the disaster of the Crusades and the lasting fallout of religious animosity would have happened without that fateful speech by an otherwise unremarkable character, Urban II. There is good evidence that Urban's audience was from the start more than inclined to go along with his exhortations. The fear and hatred between Christians and Muslims was, in the words of Daniel, "like a summer forest, ready to blaze."[13] The predisposition was there; only a trigger was required, according to what historians call the "sublimation of energy theory."

But that theory, attractive though it may seem, has one disturbing element. In its extreme form it suggests that the dynamics of history is in fact preordained, like the orbit of a planet. The actions of individual humans would merely be statistically inevitable links between what was and what, for better or worse, was to become. If Urban had not provided the spark that ignited the "summer forest," other sparks would have achieved the same end.

At the other extreme we find an equally unattractive alternative. Instead of being inevitable, history is perhaps so capricious that our destinies are tossed chaotically by the blind concurrence of accidents. Had Urban caught the flu in November of 1095, the Crusades might not have happened. The relationships between different religions and races might be entirely different today, more benevolent perhaps. Would we have been spared the Holocaust but for the minuscule chance of the person of Adolf Hitler resulting from the lovemaking of the Schueckelgrubers back in 1889?

To decide between these alternatives we would have to be able to compute the course of history. Such determinism is not applicable to human affairs. There are several reasons for this, not the least of which has to do with a process called *self-reference*. It is *our* history we are trying to compute, and having predicted it, we would be free to change it, and thus invalidate our prophecy. Questions like What would have happened, if . . . ? start with the wrong premise, that what happened did in fact *not* happen. They are *contrafactual*. Answers cannot be compared with anything that *did* happen, and are therefore gratuitous.

These reflections bring to mind an event that placed me for one brief moment at what in retrospect appears like a node in history, a point at which — with the curl of a finger — I could have unhinged the fate of nations, changed the lives of almost every human then living on earth.

When Austria was annexed by Hitler in the early spring of 1938, I was a young soldier serving in the Austrian army in the city of Graz. The *Anschluss* was generally greeted with enthusiasm by the populace; this was particularly true in that southern province of Styria of which Graz was the capital. It was perceived as reward for this support that Graz was one of the first Austrian cities visited by the Führer.

The event was carefully prepared. A detachment of my regiment, the 10th Alpine Chasseurs, was to line the street through which Hitler's motorcade would pass. We still wore Austrian uniforms, although by now we were officially part of the German army. The morning before our assignment, we were divided into two groups, odds and evens. In the single file we were to form separating the motorcade from the crowd, odds and evens alternating, the evens faced the street and the motorcade, the odds faced the crowd. The odds were instructed to watch carefully for any suspicious movement. Each had one live round in the chamber of his rifle. I was made an odd, an unforgivable oversight on the part of my company commander, who knew that I was half-Jewish.

Everything went according to schedule. We had taken our positions as instructed. I looked over the crowd. Seconds before the motorcade arrived a German lieutenant noticed a defect in the picture: at one place in the file two odds stood next to each other, which he quickly corrected with a few "about-face" commands. Soon everything looked perfect, but I stood with my loaded gun at "present-arms" facing the road as Hitler, standing in his open limousine, arm extended in the Nazi salute, slowly passed no more than ten feet in front of me.

I must confess that the thought of assassination occurred to me only years later, together with the intriguing question, What would have happened, if . . . ? Assuming that I would have been faster on the trigger than Hitler's bodyguards, would it have ended the insane path Germany was then following? If it had, nobody would have expected the averted disasters, and the event would have passed into history as just another political assassination. It is also possible that the act would only have added to the general madness, and I might have become known as "the nut who precipitated World War II and the Holocaust." Clearly, none of these What if's have any meaning.

The feeling of destiny, especially of preordained disasters, has haunted humans as far back in history as we can see. Apocalyptic thoughts were prominent throughout the Middle Ages and have again surfaced in the guise of the specter of a nuclear holocaust. The common theme is that doom is decreed for the human race, either from above or as the result of our inherent ineptitude. There is a tendency to accept and even to facilitate such a course.

Many expect the impending disaster to strike selectively. Such notions often arise from a moral elitism. Millennialist preachers have always divided mankind into the good and the evil ones, those chosen to escape and be rewarded with an eternity of bliss, and those who richly deserve the hellish fate that is in store for them.

Today's survivalists have accepted the inevitability of nuclear doom. But they feel that a submachine gun and a cache of canned soups will somehow ensure their own survival. In the meantime they romp in the Oregon woods, waiting for the rest of humanity to be vaporized.

Some of us are convinced that the nuclear holocaust will come, because — like the crowd gathered around Urban II — they believe that "it is the will of God."

The city of Amarillo, Texas, population 158,000, is the place where all nuclear weapons in the U.S. arsenal go through their final assembly. This fact contributes in no small measure to the relative prosperity of the region. The Pantex plant, where all this happens, employs about 3,000 people. One might think that such activity would place a heavy emotional burden on the community, eliciting at the very least controversy and soul-searching.

This seems not to be the case.[14] The Reverend Royce Elms, pastor of the large, fundamentalist Jubilee Tabernacle there, is a strong voice in Amarillo. "As long as we are right with God," he assures his flock, "you do not have to tear your hair out and worry about dying — if you've got blessed assurance." He predicts the end of the world "as we know it" by 1990. This new religious doctrine is known as *end time thinking*. "It's settled and sealed by the word of God," says the Reverend Mr. Elms. "I really believe God is in the control room."

In fairness it must be said that not everyone in Amarillo is sympathetic to the Reverend Mr. Elms's teachings. Some think his ideas kooky but support the nuclear weapons activity for reasons of their own. Fundamentalist feelings are, however, a strong component in the conviction of the citizens that they are doing the right thing. Amarillo, we are told, is a nice place, a "town of pleasant streets, a good place to raise a family." There is a city ordinance against fireworks.[15]

The themes of human inadequacy are repeated through history with discouraging persistence. The twentieth century has given us ample proof that we have inherited the dark passions of the Crusaders, their blind faith and convenient loyalties, their self-righteousness, their pious conviction that humanity is divided into two camps, the good and the bad, and that the bad don't merit our compassion.

But the world we have created around ourselves is very different now, much less forgiving of our shortcomings, full of knife-edge instabilities that threaten us all. Our technologies, almost with a life of their own, are racing ahead, whether we like it or not. And yet, time, which Francis Bacon called "the landscape of experience," lies before us in one piece: past, present, and future are interwoven in our minds. The boundaries that separate year from year and century from century are both arbitrary and significant, like the boundaries on a map. It is appropriate that we approach them with caution.

CHAPTER II

Evolution

To ASSESS OUR CHANCES and perhaps derive some useful guidelines for the future, we start with one of the givens, our biological nature and how it came about.

After the big bang, when our universe was formed some fifteen billion years ago, another ten billion years passed before the birth of our planet, and another two billion before the first primitive life-forms appeared. How life began is still one of the stubborn mysteries of nature, although some necessary steps have now been shown to be rather commonplace. Somewhere, the first amino acids were formed, perhaps when a bolt of lightning struck a sea rich in ammonia. It was still a long way from such precursors of the large biomolecules to the first complete living cell.

Big Bang and Little Bang

But one day, there it was in all its protoplasmic perfection, thrusting pseudopods against the viscous, barely yielding ooze into which it was born. It came complete with what the late French biochemist Jacques-

Lucien Monod called "the dream of every cell: to become two cells." And, fulfilling that dream, it divided and divided until its kith and kin had formed a colony and then another and another.

Perhaps the same process had occurred at about the same time in many places, and perhaps there were some variations at the outset. But indications are that this was a unique event, sometimes called "the little bang," one genetic plan, one successful experiment after millions of failures, and that from that fortuitous piece of DNA all of us have descended, including all the flora and fauna that ever lived.

But even though there may have been only a single genetic blueprint initially, minute changes (mutations) in the DNA must soon have led to a diversification of forms, sifted through selection by the environment. Slowly, groupings of the more viable strains appeared, and evolution was on its way.

The next biological breakthrough came when cells found it advantageous to form aggregates. Specialization of cell function within an aggregate was a natural consequence, and when the life of the colony took precedence over the life of the cell we had the beginnings of the first multicellular *organism*. The transition from individual cell to individual organism was about as revolutionary as the formation of the first cell.

The next twenty million years — a startlingly brief interval in evolutionary history — saw the emergence of the basic body designs of most major divisions in the animal kingdom. We must conclude that the great sweep of evolution that was to follow was determined, and to a very large extent constrained, by what happened in that period some six hundred million years ago. There is little doubt, also, that chance, the sheer luck or misfortune encountered by some of these early genetic experiments, altered for all future times the course of evolution.[1]

Evolution now proceeded on many fronts. Mammals appeared when the big reptiles began to decline. One line eventually led to the hominids and finally to man. The evolution of the mind is often considered the last stage in this long process and the most mysterious one.

But evolution is never a simple progression toward better forms. In fact, it makes little sense to speak of improvements in the evolution of a population or in the divergence of one species from another. Is man more adapted to his environment than an ant? Is modern man happier or better suited to his world than early man was to his?

The trail of evolution is marked by a prodigious richness, an extravagant abundance of forms. And not only the fittest survive. Evolution requires a rich pool of variants, including sports, misfits, and all the *hopeful monsters* from which, by fortuitous chance, a new viable combination may some day arise. Everything is tried, and life pushes into every nook and cranny of the environment, fills every ecological niche.

Everything is tried and much has to be abandoned. Ninety-nine percent of all species that ever lived are extinct now. The dinosaurs, the woolly mammoth, and the saber-toothed tiger didn't make it, to name only a few of the millions of evolutionary dead ends. But the happy clam has survived virtually without change for at least twenty-five million years, the opossum for eighty million years. For every species alive today, a hundred now lie frozen into the rocky sediments of the earth.

The fossils tell an eloquent story of changing forms, of species branching from other species, of successful innovations, of abandoned futile attempts, and — perhaps as remarkable as the others — of the persistence of some life-forms, virtually without change, over geologic periods. The fossil story is there for everyone to see, bearing witness to the irrefutable *fact* of evolution.

Still, Creationists will tell you that it is a *theory*, or "just a theory," as they like to put it.

Remarks like this suggest that theory represents a rather low form of information, provisional information, not yet ripened into knowledge. Instead, to the scientist theory is the ultimate goal of research; a good theory integrates and illuminates what would otherwise be just facts.

The Facts and the Theory

Facts come from diverse sources. The fossil record consists of the skeletal remains and imprints of life-forms covering enormous periods of time. The record is spotty. Unusual conditions must exist for any part of an organism to be preserved for long. But, once turned into stone, it becomes part of a stratum of rock it shares with fossils of its contemporaries of both the animal and plant world. This company will forever fix the time of its existence. It is in this way that paleontologists know about little marine creatures, the trilobites that flourished and became extinct in the Paleozoic. This is how we know about the great variety of dinosaurs that disappeared from the earth about sixty-five million years ago, and about *Aegyptopithecus*, a small apelike creature that lived about thirty-three million years ago, the oldest creature believed to have been in our direct line of ancestry. Then there are the true *hominids*, the various forms of the genus *Australopithecus*, and the three known species of *Homo*: *H. habilis, H. erectus*, and *H. sapiens*.

The fossil record is complemented by a different way scientists now have of tracing relatedness among species. In 1953 James D. Watson and Francis Crick discovered the structure of *deoxyribonucleic acid* (DNA), the molecule which contains the genetic blueprint of an organism. We now understand that the specification of every inherited trait and feature is coded into this molecule as a sequence of subunits called *nucleotides*. A stretch of nucleotides, perhaps a few hundred long, that together spell out the structure of one of the organism's many protein molecules, is called a *gene*. All of an organism's inherited characteristics are thus specified by the many genes that make up the DNA molecule.

It is now possible to compare the nucleotide sequences in DNA molecules from different species. In this way it is found, for example, that human DNA differs from that of the chimpanzee in only one percent of its nucleotides. Man and chimp are 99 percent genetically identical!

From such comparisons biologists have been able to put together a tree of relatedness and to propose a timetable for the evolution of living species from presumed common ancestors.

Is evolution then a fact, or a theory? The line between the two can not always be drawn sharply. But when facts point inescapably to certain rational conclusions, these conclusions themselves become facts. There are four processes we are thus compelled to recognize as facts; these are *conservation, modification, branching,* and *extinction*.

The first of these refers to the fact that often a species remains unchanged for long periods. There are organisms living today whose likenesses we find in layer after layer of geological deposits. We call them *living fossils*. It may seem at first that this phenomenon needs no theory, since, in fact, nothing is happening. When we realize, however, the delicate molecular processes involved in maintaining, copying, and passing on the genetic information in the form of DNA molecules, it becomes clear that preservation of exact structure over millions of years requires an explanation.

The second process, *modification,* is the centerpiece of all evolutionary theories. It asserts that life forms are generally not constant (though *some* may remain constant for long periods), and that the changes that are attributable to changes in the DNA are passed on from generation to generation.

Branching is the appearance of two distinct and diverging lines of life-forms from a common ancestor. There is powerful evidence now that humans and chimps are the end products of two lines that separated long ago, and that their common ancestor, in turn, shared a common ancestor with today's gorilla.

Finally, *extinction,* the most dramatic of the four processes, is quite simply the cessation of offspring in a dwindling population, less frequently the simultaneous destruction of a population due to catastrophic causes. Which of the two caused the demise of the dinosaurs at the end of the Cretaceous period is one of the lively disputes among biologists and paleontologists today. The plot thickened when astrophysicists entered the argument by offering evidence that the earth was pelted by enormous meteor showers at just that time.

Of the four processes, conservation, modification, branching, and extinction, the first and last were already well documented by fossil evidence in Darwin's time. Since then modification and branching have also become empirical facts.

Of course, it is always possible to invoke a set of arguments that allows one to disregard such rational conclusions. Einstein, commenting on the many puzzles of nature, and the inscrutability of some, once coined the phrase, "The Lord is subtle, but spiteful he is not." Paraphrasing Einstein, we may say that there are many barriers to our understanding of nature, but no boobytraps. To endow us with the power of reasoning and then purposely mislead us with planted fossils, would indeed be the work of a spiteful Lord.

To appreciate the passionate hostility which met Darwin's suggestion of possible modification of life-forms and the appearance of new species by branching, we must first understand *essentialism,* the entrenched philosophy in Darwin's day.

Essentialism has its roots in the philosophy of Plato, who contended that physical objects, as well as individual animals and humans, are only approximate representations of ideals: ideal tables, ideal dogs, ideal humans. Objects and individuals have only some, but not all of the *essences* of the ideals. The essential human is never encountered in the world we know. Instead, we are dealing with a great variety of individuals, imperfect facsimiles of the ideal, which has no variations and allows no change.

Our habit of *typing* other humans is derived from the philosophy of essentialism. When we speak of the *typical* Italian, Jew, German, Arab, or black, we are constructing composites that are supposedly representative of millions of individuals. In fashioning such composites we generally give free reign to our most cherished likes and dislikes. We apply typology not only to nations, ethnic groups, and religions, but also to political parties, social strata, cities, and neighborhoods. The New Jersey driver is a favorite stereotype among New Yorkers. As any New York cabbie will tell you, "They are the worst." "For the typologist," says Ernst Mayr, "everything in nature is either good or bad."[2]

Essentialism found its strongest expression in Creationism, the Judeo-Christian teaching that each species was created by divine will and remained immutable thereafter. The act of creation thus established a standard for each species, a unique, unchanging pattern that had to be reconciled with the obvious variety existing among the individuals of each species. More troubling was the fossil record, which showed, among other things, that specimens from neighboring geological periods showed greater similarity than ones from widely separated periods, and that the older the fossil the more it differed in general appearance from its living relative.

It was to account for this evident relatedness of different forms and their changing appearance through geologic history that Darwin replaced the created, immutable species by "descent with modification." From there Darwin's theory — as any theory worth its name — goes beyond the mere facts of relatedness and modification, by invoking the simplifying and illuminating idea of a common descent for all species.

It was still necessary to find an explanation for the causes and mechanisms of evolution that would be applicable to all four processes: conservation, modification, branching, and extinction. Darwin provided an answer with his principle of *natural selection*. His arguments go as follows:

Living things exhibit a fertility far beyond what is necessary to maintain a population of constant size. Given unhindered growth, this would result in a typical doubling time, and, if continued, an exponential increase in population. But populations are generally stable. This means that vast numbers of individuals don't make it to maturity. In their struggle for survival their diverse individual characteristics come into play and must make the difference between success and failure. But these characteristics are heritable, hence the population is filtered by the rigors of the environment, with a preponderance of those characteristics that spelled success.[3]

We can see, now, how these selective pressures may be responsible for the first three of the four processes that we have to explain. A simple, admittedly primitive model will illustrate the mechanisms. Consider a particular physical characteristic, say body size. In a typical population this will be distributed in something like the famous bell-shaped curve. There is the most likely size, marking the peak of the curve. Smaller or larger bodies are less likely, making the curve trail off on either side of its maximum. The so-called tails of the distribution represent the few unlikely extremes.

We begin with an explanation of conservation. Assume that the populous center of the distribution curve also marks the *best* value from the point of view of environmental adaptation. To be larger or smaller than the mean carries a disadvantage, which becomes more severe as the distance away from the mean gets larger. The high survival rate of the fittest will ensure that the population be stabilized at the present average size and maintain the peak of the distribution curve at the biologically optimal value.

Take next a situation in which the best size is not the most prevalent. It may even lie outside the distribution curve. This could have come about through environmental changes that made a previously well-adapted size obsolete. Selection will now favor specimens on one of the tails of the distribution. If a larger size is called for, the smallest specimens will be handicapped and produce fewer offspring. This will result in a progressive shifting of the distribution toward the biologically preferred values. The population will, on the average, get bigger.

Finally, it is possible that both tails of the distribution are favored. For some reason the smallest and the largest may have a better chance of surviving and reproducing than those of average size. In this scenario, the advantage conferred upon individuals at the extremes will tend to increase the frequency of these characteristics. In the course of evolution, the distribution will change from the simple bell-shaped curve to one having peaks at each end, with the middle gradually disappearing. As the two new peaks move apart, each shifted by its own adaptive requirements, the two populations may become biologically separated, representing now two different species.

Common descent and natural selection are the grand unifying principles that make up Darwin's theory of evolution. We can now understand how — in a stable environment — an adapted species can maintain itself unchanged over long periods. Natural selection will accomplish conservation by eliminating the less adapted variations as they come up. Under changing conditions the same processes will cause modifications, while branching may occur when members of a species become geographically isolated, especially if environmental conditions are very different. But branching may also occur even with separation under identical conditions, due to mutations that carry no particular advantages or disadvantages. Such neutral mutations are believed to acount for what geneticists call *genetic drift*.[4] Extinction is the ultimate breakdown of the evolutionary process: the species is overwhelmed by an environment turned hostile; adaptive processes are simply no longer able to cope.

It should be made clear that Darwin saw natural selection as a strong determinant in the evolutionary process, but not the only determinant. Much recent discussion among evolutionists concerns the degree to which evolution is governed by the environment. We must contend with the possibility that chance also shapes the path of evolution. Of course, we realize that chance plays a central role in evolution: it generates the myriad small fluctuations in our gene pool, the mutations, from which the viable combinations are selected by the environment. We often assume that the path of evolution is pretty much determined by the law of large numbers. But chance may also operate on a macroscopic scale, leaving the outcome of a particular evolutionary phase undetermined. If it were otherwise, populations that are isolated under almost identical conditions (species on neighboring islands) should evolve along very similar lines. There would be no genetic drift, and all species would tend to evolve toward an ideal or optimal design. If, on the other hand, nonselective changes played a significant role, this could account for the existence of superfluous and even deleterious traits, so-called *maladaptions*. Harvard geneticist Richard Lewontin has recently stated that "it is by no means certain, even now, what proportion of all evolutionary change arises from natural selection."[5]

We sometimes think of the evolutionary process as a series of engineering ventures, in which different designs are tried and the bad ones discarded. Every now and then, we come up with an Edsel, which is discontinued as soon as the marketing people realize the blunder.

There are analogies with natural selection but also fundamental differences. For one thing, we find that in biological evolution there is an important step missing. The new model is not *designed.* Nobody reasons out the advantages and disadvantages of a contemplated design. There are no blueprints, no calculations, no discussions between engineers and marketing experts. Genetic variations are thrown onto the stage without regard to their chances of survival, two-headed calves, Siamese twins, humans without limbs or without cerebral cortex. Many die in utero.

But some forms of detrimental design may be propagated for many generations, like the genes for sickle cell anemia, hemophilia, Tay-Sachs disease, thalassemia, and other genetic diseases. Then there are the numerous milder forms of maladaptions and the less than ideal features caused by what are called *phyletic constraints:* We mentioned already that every species shares with a large number of other species a basic design, or *bauplan.* Some of these go back hundreds of millions of years in evolutionary history and represent some unsurmountable limitations. When humans adopted their upright posture, they had to do so with a spinal chord that was less than perfectly suited to their needs. "The bipedal hominoids," Mayr points out, "are still burdened by their quadrupedal past."[6]

But the most prolific source of maladaptions is probably our own cultural evolution. This may seem strange, but only at first glance. Culture has thoroughly transformed our environment, often in ways that are incompatible with our biological needs.

The situation in engineering is not totally different. Here, too, for many practical reasons, there exists great inertia about making drastic design changes, as evidenced by the dreary similarity of successive vintages of automobiles. The appearance of tailfins and the abundant use of chromium at one stage were not unlike genetic drifts that had no adaptive advantage. But many innovations are deliberate engineering features, such as pneumatic tires, automatic shifts, or seatbelts; they are *creations,* and they appear suddenly, many without precursors.

The essence of Darwinian evolution is that life forms are not created in deliberate acts to improve functions, or to solve particular problems.

It is the uncompromising assertion of this lack of purpose that constitutes evolution's most serious break with established religion and to this day makes it unacceptable to religious fundamentalists.

The mechanism of chance mutation, which is fundamental to all evolutionary changes, also accounts for the conservative nature of evolution. To make substantial changes in design, many intermediate forms have to be gone through, and they all have to be viable. This is the meaning of phyletic constraints. There is some dispute among contemporary biologists about just how gradual these changes have to be. There appears to be a paucity of transitional forms in the fossil record, suggesting that evolution proceeded in spurts, rather than in a steady progression. But even in this *punctuated equilibrium* theory there would still be great genetic similarity between the new species and its antecedents.[7] Horses would not suddenly appear in a population of lizards.

Darwin's theory, though far from complete, has brought about ineradicable changes in the way we see ourselves. The theory of common descent, now supported by much more massive evidence than was available in Darwin's time, places the family of mankind in the midst of the larger family of all living things. The other species were not created for man's pleasure. Most of them preceded us by many millions of years. Our knowledge of universal kinship of life imparts a new flavor to the biblical injunction to rule over "every living thing that moveth upon the earth." If we have emerged with greater intelligence and power than the other beasts of the earth, this only heightens our responsibility for the preservation of *all* life, because it is our flesh and blood.

The other lesson we derive from Darwin's work has to do with the demise of essentialism. No longer is the individual a better or poorer approximation of the ideal human, or just a departure from the average man. The average is an abstraction. But a population is made up of individuals. It is the mix of all variations of body types and talents that drives the engine of evolution and makes the human family what it is.

We have not always assimilated this lesson well. There is a debate going in the backwaters of science over whether average mental characteristics differ between different racial groups. Racists take comfort from the claim that the average IQ of blacks is lower than that of whites.[8]

Leaving aside the question whether the IQ is a valid measure of native intelligence (however defined), we should not be surprised to find a difference in the computed averages of any variable, nor should this bring comfort or dismay to any group. The average man is an abstraction; he never invented a tool, wrote a poem, or painted an image. Such talents are distributed widely and liberally over all branches of the human family, but nothing assures us that they are perfectly homogenized, as though our genes were pulled out of a Waring blender. It is certainly possible that the average IQ of blacks is lower than that of Caucasians, and that they have, as the cliché goes, more rhythm (on the average). The opposite is also possible, but neither alternative should be of much consequence. We might keep in mind also that, quite possibly, the average Chinese is smarter than the average Caucasian, though few Westerners would like to see the Chinese derive sociopolitical advantages from this. It is simply not necessary to resort to dogmatic egalitarianism in order to avoid these racial dilemmas.

Modern evolutionists point out that Darwin replaced the typological approach, which places great emphasis on the collective properties of the group (the type to which an individual belongs), by *population* thinking. A type of population is not a population of types, but of individuals. This was as radical a departure from pre-Darwinian thinking as the theory of common descent. The full impact of this change has yet to be assimilated. I will suggest later that some of our present societal problems can be attributed to a substantial residue of typological thinking.

Today the theory of evolution is still a rather loose assembly of widely scattered facts, some brilliant deductions, many conjectures, and many controversies and shifting opinions. It has not achieved, and probably never will achieve, the compactness or the precision of some of the great physical theories, such as Newton's theory of gravitation, or Einstein's theory of special relativity. It is in the nature of evolutionary theory to be, in a sense, open-ended. We sometimes feel that we understand the processes so well that we are ready to wrap it all up in a neat set of equations. And then we think some more, and we feel lost again.

This incompleteness and some notable controversies are often cited by religious fundamentalists as fatal flaws in the theory of evolution. They are not. If anything, they add to the excitement, the intellectual ferment that marks activity in this area. We must also keep in mind that underlying the conjectures and the hand-waving arguments, there are facts as hard as any others found in the sciences: the gradual changing and branching of species, the descent of contemporary species, such as humans and apes, from earlier common ancestors. Modern paleobiology allows us to trace back the different lineages through the long sweep of evolution and reconstruct the general features of a tree of life that is rooted in the most ancient and primitive organisms. None of this can be ignored by anyone who values his or her powers of reasoning.

Chimps and Early Hominids

"At one point . . . the traveler stops, pauses, turns to the left to glance at some possible threat or irregularity, then continues to the North." This from Mary Leakey's account of a set of footprints immortalized in rock and found at Laetoli, in Tanzania, not far from the Olduvai Gorge.[6] The traveler had walked across a stretch of soft volcanic ash about 3.7 million years ago. The imprints are perfectly preserved and barely distinguishable from tracks made by contemporary humans. The traveler walked erect, with a gait that was, in Mary Leakey's description, "intensely human." He or she belonged to the genus *Australopithecus,* an early hominid, very likely in our direct line of descent or close to it, but with a brain barely larger than an ape's. A few well-preserved fossils allow us to look back at these remote ancestors with both wonderment and a sense of familiarity: there is a beautifully preserved front of a two-million-year-old skull of a child — known as the Taung child — and Lucy, the nearly complete skeleton of a mature woman who lived between three and four million years ago.

Australopithecus afarensis, the species to which Lucy belonged, lasted for something like a million years. It is one of a number making up the genus *Australopithecus.* We call them the australopithecines. They were true bipeds, as the Laetoli tracks so eloquently show. This faculty, which would have been useless in the tropical forest, was clearly of great adaptive advantage on the open savannah where they lived. Their hands, freed from the task of locomotion, could now be used to carry food, their young, and perhaps material for a shelter.

According to another theory, proposed by Walter M. Bortz II, the ability of early man to cover large distances swiftly was due to the fact that his erect posture diminished the heat load from solar radiation, while the absence of body hair (presumed) and the prodigious distribution of sweat glands over most of his body greatly increased his capacity for extended physical exertion. These factors, according to Bortz, enabled early hunters (as well as some contemporary aborigines) to "hunt down" the swiftest quadrupeds and kill the exhausted prey virtually without weapons.[10]

But it is not clear just what adaptive pressures caused the transition from four-footedness to bipedalism. The controversy goes on among anthropologists over whether the new mobility or the new dexterity conferred the more significant advantages.

It has also been argued that — unlike apes, who fight with their teeth — the hands, aided perhaps by a rock or club, had now become the dominant mode of defense or aggression of the australopithecines. Evolution seems to act on a principle of parsimony: the prominent and powerful canine teeth of the apes have been replaced by a set of teeth very similar to those of modern humans.

The australopithecines certainly were users, but probably not makers of tools. In this respect they were not so different from today's chimpanzees. Jane Goodall, who has observed these creatures in the wild, tells us how chimps use blades of grass to extract termites from their mounds,[11] and the Dutch zoologist Adriaan Kortlandt provided us with pictures of a forest chimpanzee attacking a dummy leopard with a club.

The early hominids and today's chimpanzees thus appear at similar stages of brain evolution, and exhibit similar faculties. It has been suggested, but not demonstrated, that colonies of wild chimpanzees may have developed cultural differences, and that Jane Goodall's colony is perhaps as different from others as people in Marin County are from inhabitants of Borneo.[12]

But chimpanzees differ from the australopithecines in at least one important aspect: they can rear up on their hind legs to fight and walk bipedally for short distances, but, unlike their hominid cousins, they are not able to cover any great distances this way.

Biologists have been surprised by the intelligence chimpanzees exhibit when in captivity. They readily develop faculties not observed, and perhaps useless, in the wild. They are our favorite animal performers because of their near-human appearance. They are able to learn and use an impressive repertory of signals, which some biologists have interpreted as language.[13] Konrad Lorenz gives us this description of a chimpanzee in captivity, contemplating a banana that was attached to the ceiling of a room, just out of reach. The room also contained a box:

> The matter gave him no peace, and he returned to it again. Then, suddenly — and there is no other way to describe it — his previously gloomy face "lit up." His eyes now moved from the banana to the empty space beneath it on the ground, from this to the box, then back to the space, and from there up to the banana. The next moment he gave a cry of joy, and somersaulted over to the box in sheer high spirits. Completely assured of his success, he pushed the box below the banana. No man watching him could doubt the existence of a genuine "Aha" experience in anthropoid apes.[14]

We have mentioned before the astonishing genetic closeness between man and chimp as revealed by direct comparison of their DNA molecules. Such a relationship exists, to a lesser extent, also between man and gorilla. But the same research shows that the chimpanzee is closer to man than to the gorilla.[15]

Adriaan Kortlandt has come up with an intriguing theory concerning the interaction of australopithecines and chimpanzees, or their presumed ancestors. According to this *dehumanization theory,* the two species at one time coexisted and competed for living space on the African grasslands, but the clearly superior hominids eventually drove the chimps back into the forest and back into a more primitive existence. Thus dehumanized, they nevertheless retained through the ages an intelligence beyond their needs and their station in the animal kingdom.

The anthropologist Richard Alexander (University of Michigan) speculates that "if by some chance the human species should be extinguished while the chimpanzees are not, there is a fair chance that chimpanzees would embark upon an evolutionary path paralleling in some important regards that taken by human ancestors across the past million years or so."[16]

This version is compatible with the image of early hominids as fearsome brutes, "killer apes," as the anthropologist Raymond Dart described them. More recent accounts paint a kinder image of our ancestors. Some of the australopithecines may have been vegetarians; others, still lacking the tools to be efficient hunters, may have shared with hyenas and other scavengers the remains of kills left by the big cats.

Killer ape, scavenger, or harmless herbivore, it is doubtful that the australopithecines had mastered the art of making stone tools by deliberately chipping away at a native rock. This faculty had to wait for *Homo habilis,* the "handy man," and *Homo erectus,* his successor. Both of these species showed pronounced increase in body and brain size over the earlier hominids.

Probably the most complete fossil skeleton of Stone Age man is that of the Boy of Nariokotome, found in 1984 in Kenya by Alan Walker and Richard Leakey. It belonged to a member of *Homo erectus,* a boy aged about twelve years at time of death. It is estimated that — had he grown to maturity — he would have stood six feet tall and had a brain capacity of about 882 cubic centimeters, still 500 cubic centimeters short of that of modern man but significantly higher than that of the australopithecines.[17]

It would be fascinating to speculate just why the genus *Homo* was able to accomplish what his predecessors failed to do: develop an industry of toolmaking. It seems unlikely that the earlier hominids simply had not stumbled on the trick of chipping flakes off stones. Chance, to be sure, plays a larger role than we like to admit in the course of cultural evolution. The Mayas of Central America had a high civilization lasting for centuries and never invented the wheel.

But to have failed for a million years to take what seems now such an obvious next step strains the laws of probability. We must conclude instead that *Australopithecus* was unable to do it. This inability may have had something to do with limited manual dexterity. We know that in the evolving hominid brain increasing portions of cerebral cortex are dedicated to the control of hand movements. Still, it seems that even the chimp would have had sufficient muscular control, and certainly enough strength in his fingers, to accomplish the job.

This suggests that toolmaking necessitates mental faculties not possessed by the more primitive creatures. By "toolmaking" we now mean the manufacture of implements sufficiently standardized for us to recognize the stage of human evolution that produced them. This implies socialization and communication and the development of relatively stable traditions that are generally associated with a culture.

But the real obstacle to earlier development of toolmaking was probably not lack of muscle control or communication skills, but the inability of the more primitive brain to conceive of the process.

Let us see what is involved. Imagine yourself on the African savannah back in the waning days of the australopithecines, of whom you are one, and the first appearance of the genus *Homo*. You are faced with a certain task, say the dismemberment of a large carcass for the purpose of carrying the pieces back to your lair. You struggle, using tooth and claw and perhaps sticks and stones. You may, if you are lucky, stumble on the property of sharpness found in some piece of flint accidentally broken. You may even remember that event and smash a rock next time you face a similar job. But you have not yet crossed the threshold of the true toolmaker. For that you have to envision something that does not yet exist: a cutting edge formed not by one accidental or intentional fracture but by a series of deliberate acts of chipping. This requires the brain to sample and manipulate mental images, judge their usefulness, and then direct the hands to turn into reality what the mind has conceived.[18]

But your brain is a few hundred cubic centimeters short of being able to accomplish this. And so your kind will go down in prehistory as one that had to give way to another race, which was taller and smarter and was at last able to give birth to civilization.

CHAPTER III

The Evolution of Culture

THEY MADE THEIR FIRST appearance in the early, the so-called lower, Pleistocene. The genus *Homo* was taller than its australopithecine contemporaries and showed the first significant advance in brain size over the apes: an increase of 50 percent. It was enough to break the million-year deadlock. Man began to make tools.

The further growth of the brain in the evolution of *Homo* — *Homo habilis, Homo erectus*, and the different forms of *Homo sapiens* — was nothing short of spectacular. We must assume that the higher functions of the central nervous system had suddenly assumed paramount significance in the survival game and had thus taken control of the evolutionary process.

There are other examples in the history of the animal kingdom of such takeovers by single body characteristics: the size of the canines of the sabertooth tigers, the size of the antlers of the Irish elk, or the sheer bulk of some dinosaurs. Such examples gave rise to an earlier evolutionary theory, called *orthogenesis,* according to which such singular properties with overwhelming adaptive advantage may lead to an evolutionary cul-de-sac. An adaptive feature will develop out of all proportions until all evolutionary gains have been wrung from it. A point of no return is reached when the species has thus exhausted its adaptability. It is now vulnerable to further changes in environment and will eventually perish as an anachronism of evolution.

The theory of orthogenesis has been generally discredited in biological evolution but may well apply to *cultural* evolution, where it may produce a "drive toward extinction."[1] Our present nuclear standoff, with its escalating arsenal of offensive and defensive weaponry, may be a case in point. If no safe way of disarming can be found — and this is still the claim of many military advisors — then the (apparent) advantages gained from further armaments will continue to propel us along what may be called an orthocultural one-way path to oblivion.

Is brain evolution still continuing among humans, and should we be concerned about an orthogenetic disaster? The image of a future superrace of humans with grotesquely enlarged craniums supported by wizened bodies has for long been the stuff of science fiction as well as of some serious scientific speculation.

Predictions in science are often gratuitous and are rarely on the mark. Nevertheless, we can say that — looking over the past 100,000 years or so — we see no significant changes in stature, or in general appearance, including brain size, in our species. This is not to say that mutations no longer occur in the human genome. But we observe no trends that would systematically transform the human image.

It has been said that modern *Homo sapiens,* and perhaps even his more primitive cousin the Neanderthal, could, if appropriately dressed, walk down Fifth Avenue in New York without attracting attention.

The question of brain evolution is, of course, a subtle one, and 100,000 years is not a long interval on the evolutionary clock. We have only overall size and a few incomplete casts of skull interiors to go on, apart from the more durable artifacts that were left behind. It is possible, therefore, that evolutionary changes in brain structure since that time, though not evident in the fossil record, have gone on apace with the spectacular evolution of human culture.

It would be tempting to say that the rapidly changing tasks and problems that came with cultural changes brought in new adaptive criteria to which genetic evolution responded. This is the thesis of what Charles J. Lumsden and Edward O. Wilson have called *gene-culture coevolution.*[2] We may think that such intellectual accomplishments as the sophisticated use of language or the ability to prove mathematical theorems require subtleties of brain structure for which our Cro-Magnon ancestors would have had no use and which would not have arisen without prompting by necessity.

The most plausible example of gene-culture coevolution is the rapid growth of brain size starting with *Homo habilis* and ending with the appearance of our own species, *Homo sapiens*. This evolutionary phenomenon is most readily explained as a kind of bootstrap process, in which the first such changes engender profound behavioral changes (culture), which in turn makes larger brains progressively more advantageous.

Lumsden and Wilson, in a book called *Promethean Fire*, suggest that "some of the genetic advance in symbolic reasoning and language could have occurred during the past 50,000 years, or less. It might be continuing right into historical times."[3]

We have little evidence for or against this supposition, and it may equally be asserted that no significant genetic changes have taken place in our brain structure or organization in the past 50,000 to 100,000 years.

There are even some indications that the advanced skills mentioned above are *not* the result of further subtle genetic changes in the human brain, but that our Paleolithic ancestors came fully equipped with a twentieth-century brain, or something close to it.

To test this assertion we would need a time machine to take us back to the upper Pleistocene to kidnap an infant *Homo sapiens* and ship him back into the present before the troop of irate Cro-Magnons catches up with us. The infant, young enough to be still untouched by Paleolithic culture, must then be reared in our technological society and given our standard primary and secondary education, complete with literature, mathematics, and piano lessons — and watched. If he or she then performs as well as the average contemporary child, we will have proven the point. In the absence of a time machine we would have to do the next-best thing. There still exist on our planet a few pockets of Stone Age cultures that anthropologists are eagerly studying. There is no guarantee, of course, that they are genetically comparable to prehistoric Stone Age man. But this is not necessary to make a point here. If, in fact, it could be shown that an infant from, say, the !Kung San tribe of the Kalahari desert in Africa, brought up in Western society, could readily adapt to meet all the intellectual requirements of our technological culture, then it would be evident that the *genetic* prerequisites were there all the time and *had not evolved in response to specific needs.*

There are stories of just such cases, but, to my knowledge, they are all anecdotal. We have, however, the report of one study on !Kung San infants, according to which all cerebral reflexes appear to be the same as those of babies of our own culture.[4] To be sure, this does not exclude the kind of subtle neurological differences that Lumsden and Wilson suggest, but it goes considerably beyond simple comparisons of brain size.

If it turns out, as I very much suspect, that our aboriginal infant does well in our technological culture, then he possesses a remarkable gift of adaptation. He is able to adjust mentally and physically to a wide range of environments and develop in his lifetime skills that none of his forebears ever had the opportunity to exercise.

The Promethean Gene

We are then left with this puzzle: if the brain of the !Kung San infant has latent abilities that could not have evolved in response to adaptive pressures, then there seems to be no need to assume that what prepared *us* for this technological age was culture-induced "genetic advances" during recent millennia. We might as well assume that there existed in the brain of prehistoric man, like the invisible images on an undeveloped film, the latent abilities to carry out functions that would not find expression for many thousands of years. By what strange principle of evolution did they get there?

This question was raised by early evolutionists, and is used still by Creationists, as an argument for a separate creation of man. The answer given most frequently now is that adaptability is itself a genetic trait.

Adaptation, defined by the Harvard evolutionary biologists Stephen J. Gould and Richard C. Lewontin as "the good fit of organisms to their environment,"[5] comes in three forms: *genetic* adaptation is the slow evolutionary change of genetic material in response to environmental requirements. Such changes, of course, are heritable; *cultural* adaptation comprises shifts in customs, language, technology — to name only a few examples — characteristic of a particular society or culture. These changes are heritable also, but in a different sense. We inherit the cultural capital of our civilization only by virtue of growing up and living within this culture. It is not in our genes. Finally, there is *individual* adaptation — our ability to adjust body functions and characteristics, as well as mental processes, during our lifetimes, as the need arises. Our muscles become stronger as we use them, our hands become callused after periods of hard labor, and we learn to cope with emotional setbacks.

Although cultural and individual adaptation cause no genetic changes, our ability to adapt is a genetically conferred gift. A genetic change may cause an increased adaptability, that is, greater flexibility to changing environmental demands. It is in the nature of humans to become mathematicians, astronomers, craftsmen as the need arises, but individual genetic differences confer on each of us greater or lesser gift and inclination in one direction or another. This is not to say that some of us are necessarily born to be mathematicians. (I will come back to the nature-nurture controversy later in this chapter and in later chapters.) Let us just say that in each of our infants there may exist the latent ability to become scientist, merchant, president, or thief.

If, then, the !Kung San infant has these same latent abilities — and I firmly believe that he does — then this outstanding gift of adaptation must be a genetic characteristic of humans. It has been called the *Promethean gene.* I propose that it must have developed somewhere along the line of the genus *Homo,* and been completed by the time *Homo sapiens* appeared. Perhaps the rapid climatic changes during the Pleistocene — ice ages alternating with warm interglacial periods — constituted the first nudge toward greater adaptability. The evolutionary solution was more brain, greater inventiveness, higher intelligence.[6] Humans must have begun to contemplate more profoundly their own circumstances, ponder their past and draw conclusions, envision the future and make plans. And, most importantly, they must have developed the ability to exchange these thoughts with other humans.

Before the Pleistocene was over, and before a new geologic age marked the transition from Paleolithic to Neolithic cultures, humans had acquired a mind. It was perhaps evolution's last gift, before a runaway civilization made it impossible for genetic changes to keep pace with an environment that was driven by civilization itself. This transition from slow genetic evolution to a mind-driven, or cultural, evolution, is yet another revolutionary step in the history of life on earth. It sets us apart from the rest of the animal kingdom in a way that was hinted at by the fifteenth-century mystic Pico della Mirandola. In a passage from his "Oration on the Dignity of Man," Pico describes God's final act of creation:

> Taking man, therefore, this creature of indeterminate image, He set him in the middle of the world and thus spoke to him: "We have given you, oh Adam, no visage proper to yourself, nor any endowment properly your own, in order that whatever place, whatever form, whatever gifts you may, with premeditation, select, these same you may have and possess through your own judgment and decision. The nature of all other creatures is defined and restricted within laws which We have laid down; you, by contrast, impeded by no such restrictions, may, by your own free will, to whose custody We have assigned you, trace for yourself the lineament of your own nature. I have placed you at the very center of the world, so that from that vantage point you may with greater ease glance round about you on all that the world contains."[7]

We speak of a Promethean gene, but of course it is not *one* gene that placed at our disposal this gift to "trace . . . the lineament of [our] own nature." It is rather the addition of a few hundred cubic centimeters of brain matter. But here we encounter another strange puzzle. The approximately threefold increase in brain size from *Australopithecus* to *Homo sapiens* is accomplished at what appears to be minimal genetic cost.

We have already described how all genetic information is contained in DNA, a minute molecular chain in which individual links are strung together like letters in a word. The links are called *nucleotides*, and there are just four different types. The genetic alphabet has four letters, but the DNA message is made up of billions of letters. Thus, a lot of information is packed into the DNA molecules. In fact, if we could read the whole message, it would tell us everything about our body structure, the enzymes and hormones that drive us and urge us along. It would also give us a complete plan of our nervous system.

From a comparison of human and chimpanzee DNA biologists have determined that the two blueprints are virtually identical.[8] They differ in only about one percent of their nucleotide sequences. This small difference must account for some obvious differences in appearance between man and chimpanzee. This leaves less than 1 percent of the human genome to specify the additional brain mass. Some of the changes there are quite specific: the greatly enlarged neural centers that control hand movements and give humans their unique manual dexterity and new brain areas, such as Broca's bulge, which is concerned with speech. But the enormous increase in brain size, the addition of billions of neurons making trillions of delicate connections, the synapses that weave the neurons into a functioning communications network — all that is accomplished with a startlingly small amount of additional genetic information. It is as though the evolutionary command was simply: add more brain. And never mind the details.

But this topic is full of contradictions, and we must add a word of caution here. Brain mass is not everything. We have learned that among today's humans there is almost as much variation in brain size as there is in height or body weight, and that neither is a reliable indicator of intelligence. The average male brain is several hundred grams larger than that of the average female, which should delight male chauvinists until they hear the rest of the story. The brain of a whale is enormous compared with any human's. But then all of the whale is enormous, and if we take the ratio of brain weight to body weight we find that to be much smaller than man's. If we arrange animal species according to that ratio (rather than absolute brain size), our species comes out on top where we believe it belongs. But now we find that women are ahead of men. And so it goes.

Disease makes it necessary in some unfortunate cases to remove surgically an entire hemisphere of the human brain. This reduces the remaining brain mass of the individual to that of *Homo habilis,* the lowest of our genus. Yet often the patient suffers almost no loss of function and continues to perform normally on IQ tests.[9]

I mention all this to make clear that we are far from understanding how brains function and how they account for our unique gifts. It is undeniable, however, that, whatever changes occurred between australopithecines and the genus *Homo,* the outcome was not just another hominid but an entirely different kettle of fish. This last known step in our genetic evolution brought forth the human mind. This single concept denotes, among many other things, a new principle in the equation of survival, and, for the rest of the animal kingdom, the most formidable reordering of the power structure of the biological universe. For mankind and its emerging culture, the impact was beyond anything that could have been anticipated.

Prehistory

Unlike his forebears, who were confined to the African continent, *Homo erectus* left traces of his existence in all parts of the Old World: advanced stone tools in Africa, evidence of mass hunts in Spain (in which he apparently used grass fires to drive herds of elephants over cliffs); the remnants of huts (the first known constructed human habitations) in southern France, and in China, about one and a half million years ago, the charred bones of animals, attesting to his controlled use of fire and the habit of roasting meat (including apparently that of other humans).

Did *Homo erectus* speak? Melvin Konner, author, anthropologist, and physician, considers it likely that fire provided a strong focus for nightly gatherings, the recounting of hunting adventures, perhaps the first fisherman's tall tales.[10] But the record unfortunately is mute on the subject of human speech. Fossil brain casts are inadequate to answer the question. At best they may tell us whether certain brain centers we consider essential for speech have developed. They do not tell us to what extent, if any, *Homo erectus* actually used language. Conjectures abound.

Anthropologists have tried to argue that advanced toolmaking is evidence for mental faculties that must surely include speech. The point is sometimes made that both are complex and sequential operations, and that a brain that is capable of one should also be able to do the other.

Thomas Wynn, an anthropologist at the University of Colorado, has recently pointed out that this is a weak argument. Linguistic faculty, Wynn states, cannot be surmised from the status of toolmaking industry.[11]

But perhaps there is an indirect way of arguing for a talking *Homo erectus*. We may ask by what means the elaborate techniques of toolmaking were able to develop and spread. At a certain stage of the art, merely seeing the final product may not have sufficed for reproducing the axe head, the spearpoint, or the procedure for making fire. A student would have to observe the entire process of fabrication and be shown certain tricks by the master. But that is slow, and we may wonder how such knowledge could spread across continents, given the thinness of the population and the relative isolation of groups. The word could be crucial here, and the need to tell must have been felt acutely by these early artisans. Of course, it is possible that language existed already among the earlier *Homo habilis*, whose only tool was the primitive hand axe. We just don't know and may never know.

There is little doubt, however, that there must have been sophisticated communication among the Neanderthals, whose stone technology went far beyond that of *Homo erectus*. Not only did they produce a much greater variety of tools, but the steps involved in the manufacture became both more elaborate and more efficient. The Levallois technique, named after a Paleolithic site near Paris, consisted of taking a large piece of flint, or nodule, and first trimming it to the desired outline of the intended tools. One end of the stone was then shaped into a narrow, flat striking platform. With a soft hammer (made of bone) it was then possible to strike off a whole series of flakes, each of which became the blank for an entire new tool.

This technique was extensively used throughout Neanderthal cultures of western Europe. In the expanding tool kit of that time we also find the first bone needles with eyes, attesting to the manufacture of clothing from hides, and harpoon heads made of antlers. The relative uniformity of artifacts, which archaeologists refer to as the *Mousterian culture* (named after the town of Moustier, France), is difficult to reconcile with the low population density. Estimates are that in all of France there were no more than a few thousand humans at one time and that they were scattered into small groups that encountered each other only on rare occasions.[12]

The Neanderthals stepped onto the stage of prehistory well over 100,000 years ago. They disappeared rather suddenly — within a 5000-year span — somewhere between 30,000 and 40,000 years ago.

A much maligned race when anthropologists first encountered their remains, we have learned more and more to respect them. Certainly, they were powerfully built, with sloping foreheads and protruding brow ridges. But they were not the lumbering, dim-witted brutes they were once made out to have been. Their brain size was perhaps larger, certainly equal to that of modern man's. They are now classified by some as belonging to our own species, *Homo sapiens,* subspecies *neanderthalensis.*

They were thrust into a harsh environment. European winters during this last of the Ice Ages were long and brutal, and survival must have taken heroic efforts in both physical stamina and ingenuity. Nevertheless, the same people were the first to bury their dead and to evolve a social structure that provided support and protection to their aged and infirm. We cannot otherwise explain the presence of skeletal remains that show advanced age and debilitating chronic diseases.

With the coming of the Neanderthals man began to employ ritual, perhaps even developed beliefs in magic, all of which seem to have centered around their practices of burying the dead. Graves were dug, and the corpses were laid to rest in a gently relaxed position, as though sleeping on their sides, with legs drawn up slightly and head resting on the right arm. Tools and food were frequently placed next to the dead, sometimes the heads of bears, in what was evidently a cult of some sort. One dead youth was buried on a bed of flowers some sixty thousand years ago.[13]

It is difficult to avoid the notion that the Neanderthals believed in an afterlife. They left nothing we could call even the beginnings of art — with one possible exception: over the burial site of a young child at La Ferrassie, in France, was placed a long flat stone that bears on the side facing the skeleton pairs of small, cup-shaped depressions, cut deliberately with a pointed flint tool. Some anthropologists believe they represent human breasts and may have been symbolic of motherhood, fertility, or even a new life.[14] If this stone can be counted as representational art, it is the oldest such example.

Neanderthals seem to have had more in common with modern humans, the more we learn about them. Anthropologists now consider them part of the species *Homo sapiens,* although they show distinct anatomical differences. The last significant evolutionary changes in our family tree occurred probably well over one hundred thousand, and perhaps as much as three hundred thousand, years ago, with the appearance of a new subspecies, *Homo sapiens sapiens,* the first truly modern humans.

The place and exact time of their first appearance are unknown. The manner in which modern humans diverged from their predecessors — probably *Homo erectus* — is in some dispute, which has profound implications for the relationship between peoples of today.

Long before modern man appeared, *Homo erectus* had populated most of the Old World from Africa, across Europe, and over most of Asia. According to one theory, *Homo sapiens sapiens*, sometimes called *modern Homo sapiens*, evolved independently and more or less simultaneously in many locations of this vast area. Such parallel evolutionary processes could easily have led to considerable genetic differences in the emerging populations, perhaps even separation into different species. To explain the continued coherence of the human species, it is assumed in this theory that contact had been maintained across the perimeters of the scattered groups, and that the resulting gene flow between them helped maintain a semblance of homogeneity.

The alternative theory of *single origin*, also called *Noah's Ark theory*, assumes that the transformation of *Homo erectus* into modern *Homo sapiens* occurred at a single location somewhere in Africa. From there, the new species spread into the Eurasian landmass just as *Homo erectus* did before them.

In the first picture, modern humans can be viewed as different races, whose evolutionary histories — apart from the equalizing effects of gene flow — have been different over long periods of time and may even have started from genetically dissimilar subspecies of earlier hominids. Equality of the races would then at best be fortuitous and could certainly not be taken for granted. This point is emphasized by recent calculations showing that gene flow must have been a very slow process, considering the sparsity of the population and the vast distances involved.[15] By contrast, the theory of single origin suggests a more unified family of humans.

Strong evidence in favor of a single origin was cited recently by C. B. Stringer and P. Andrews, two paleontologists at the British Museum.[16] They pointed out that studies of human DNA showed remarkably small variations in the genetic material from person to person and even smaller differences between the averages of widely separated ethnic groups. Humans are closer to one another than are members of a single subspecies of gorilla. According to Stringer and Andrews the multiple location theory of human history is not compatible with this high degree of genetic homogeneity.

The controversy is by no means settled. Even the single origin thesis of human evolution still does not adequately explain the fact of our genetic unity. Other species that had groups living in relative isolation evolved features that adapted them to local environments, like Darwin's famous finches of the Galapagos Islands. Such *adaptive radiations* eventually lead to *speciation,* when interbreeding is no longer possible between the diverging subspecies. But, although humans have inhabited the most diverse climates, some for long periods of time and in relative isolation, no significant adaptive radiations have appeared. It was pointed out that this attests to the unequalled sociability of humans and to the fact that their adaptations are behavioral, rather than biological.[17] The manufacture of tools, the use of fire and animal furs, are skills that can be traded through complex social networks, and thus preempt the need for slow genetic changes.

Art is the creation of modern man. It appears suddenly and in profusion, the work of Cro-Magnon man, representatives of *Homo sapiens sapiens* living in southern France about thirty thousand years ago. At that time they began to decorate countless caves in France and in Spain with the images of bison, mammoths, ibex, deer, galloping horses, rhinos, and occasionally a human figure. What caused people to create these magnificent images? What changes in their brains made it possible for them to do so?

On the rugged coast of Portugal, near the fishing village of Peniche, there is a rock known to locals as *the Madonna.* With a little imagination — I had to turn my head this way and that way for a while — you can make out a seated female figure silhouetted against the sky. Similarly, on the coast of Corsica, a recumbent lion can be seen, sculpted in stone by wind and waves, and nearby a very convincing head of an old man, face pinched, with a thin, pointed nose and receding gums. We have all watched clouds and seen them assume a variety of animal shapes. Such fortuitous likenesses may have given humans the idea of making images.[18] Perhaps it was the other way around, that only after having experimented with imitating nature with stone, bone, pigment, or clay, have we been able to appreciate the many accidental shapes around us.

Whichever it is, the ability to spot resemblances is uniquely human. It is another faculty that came with the brain of modern man. We tend to take this gift for granted, and we are often amazed that animals are so unmoved by pictures, even when to us they seem perfect likenesses. We fail to appreciate how unlifelike even a color movie must seem to a dog. It does not smell, it has no depth, and — worst of all — it does not respond to anything you do to it.

Our ability to perceive and make images must be seen, therefore, as a special and valuable gift. Art and science are both offspring of these same unique faculties.

The connection between object and image (accidental or intended) must have been an exciting discovery for man. Long before humans fashioned the magnificent murals of Lascaux or Altamira, they must have thrilled at how a line scratched in the sand could be made to look like a face or an animal. Long before cave art had developed a style, as recognizable as any in the history of art, and long before a purpose arose for these expressions — whatever that purpose was — humans must have experimented with line and form, clumsily at first, but for the sheer joy of discovery.

This playtime may have lasted for many centuries. We must keep in mind also that all art is abstraction — think again of the dog who will not recognize the most realistic painting. It is not surprising, therefore, that the processes of abstraction, reduction, and stylization became themselves the objectives in art at a very early stage.

Denis Vialou, archaeologist at the Paris Institute of Human Paleontology, who has studied cave paintings in the Ariège Valley of the Pyrenees, remarked that these artists "knew their animals down to the finest detail, and were perfectly capable of drawing striking likenesses. We must assume that every incomplete figure, every ambiguous or imaginary figure, was drawn that way with a purpose."[19]

The difficulties the cave artists encountered — and sought out — were almost beyond description. Painting with only the sputtering light of animal fat burning in a stone lamp, they had to draw all images from memory. The underground chambers were inaccessible to any of the animals depicted in the paintings. Entrance was often through barely manageable crawl space, sometimes over steep rock walls requiring a mountain climber's skill. J. E. Pfeiffer describes the Nerja cave on the southern coast of Spain:

> Lya Dams, a Belgian investigator trained at the University of Toulouse, is studying the cave with her husband Marcel, who discovered the place after some intrepid climbing. The way in calls for scaling a 45-foot wall, inch-by-inch scrambling and crawling, searching for footholds and handholds, up a slippery limestone flow. . . . At the far end, blocking direct access to deeper places, is a huge stalagmite column, and the only way to get around it is by a careful straddling

maneuver — by hugging tight, stretching a foot over a sheer drop to a ledge on the other side, and pulling yourself across. That brings you into a recess where you stoop and crawl, then turn over on your back to see more abstract forms, a long-necked hind, a red ibex, and a fish. Incidentally, there are paintings on that stalagmite — on the sheer-drop side, of course. Somehow a prehistoric artist managed to suspend himself over the edge long enough to paint a black stag there and a large red spot.[20]

But nothing could have prepared you for the explosion of color and movement, as you watch the silent procession of prehistoric beasts across the walls of the great gallery of Lascaux: bison, bulls, rhinos, ibex, wild horses, and deer, all drawn with the gravity of illustrations for a children's fairy tale.

Some of the creations are obvious flights of fantasy, like the strangely twisted, almost heraldic-looking antlers of the stags, or the beast with the polka-dotted body and two straight horns. André Leroi-Gourhan, one of the outstanding students of Paleolithic art and former director of the Musée de L'Homme in Paris, describes it as "a consciously created monster: not a composite one like the griffin or the winged bull, but a monster in which every semblance of reality is deliberately violated."[21] But most are drawn with a stark realism, like the giant bulls, the galloping horses, or the herd of deer fording a stream.

We ask again: Why did they do it? Granted that humans had evolved the ability to spot resemblances, to create likenesses — why did these people, whose existence was at best precarious, spend the time and effort, pour such passion into an endeavor that produced neither food nor shelter nor safety?

There is a consensus among archaeologists that Lascaux and the other painted caves of that period represent sanctuaries, that is, places where rituals of some kind were performed. These caves were not habitations but places visited. We can only guess — and there are many guesses — as to what rites may have taken place there: fertility, puberty, celebration of the seasons, or shamanistic rituals connected with the hunt. The last is suggested because hunting is a frequent theme depicted in the paintings, and because of its obvious importance in the lives of Paleolithic people. Other interpretations have ranged from religious to Freudian to Marxist. Some features seem to suggest a theme, but the code, if there is a code, has not been broken.

Perhaps there was dancing in the caves; some ancient footprints suggest that. There are remnants of musical instruments: "hipbone xylophone, skull and shoulderblade drums, and jawbone castanets," also flutes made of bone.[22] If the caves served to hold festivals, then what was the function of the paintings that can be seen by only one person at a time and at great peril? Any unifying theme that has been proposed seems to be contradicted by some feature.

Nevertheless, whatever purpose or lore was behind the art of the upper Paleolithic, one message emerges about the nature of Cro-Magnon man. The talent of seeing images and of constructing like-nesses, which must have started as playful exploration, was pursued here with single-minded intensity. Every limit was explored and boundaries were pushed back. Whatever other motivations may have existed, there was behind cave art the drive to excel, the adventure, the challenge of breaking out of the mold of the past and attempting the impossible. In this Cro-Magnon revealed his most human trait, that of defying classifications and restrictions, which Pico della Miran-dola has so clearly pointed out.

Humans have continued to do just that ever since. Unlike animals, which tend to remain in their ecological niches until forced out, hu-mans have always contested the limits of their vision, their knowledge, and their physical strength.

This expansionist character of the human spirit has a powerful an-tagonist in the drive to preserve the status quo, to block advance, even to return to a previous condition. There is no contradiction in this. Human emotions come in pairs, as do the hormones that engender them: love and hate; joy and sadness; hope and despair. Similarly, our adventuresome spirit is often balanced by the strong emotional pull of the past, and we are torn between ambition and nostalgia.

We often view the past as idyllic and morally superior to the present, but out of reach. In the Bible story, paradise was a place of simple delights, life was innocent, indolent, and eternal. The Roman poet Ovid described the classical myth of the Golden Age as a period in which people lived without fear within fixed and secure boundaries. Nobody felt the need to travel. There was no military, no need for weapons, no strife of any kind. People did the right thing without being threatened by laws, and they had faith. Fields needed no ploughing, but food was plentiful and chosen without artifice. The rivers flowed with milk and honey.[23]

Such fantasies of prehistory could not have been farther from the truth. Satisfaction with one's lot was never a human trait in the best of times, and times were never that good. As we have seen, the earliest of the hominids were innovators, and we may have to go back in our family tree to *Ramapithecus,* or farther, before we find a creature that was "defined and restricted" within recognizable laws.

But our drive to conserve does not just produce idle nostalgia. It makes us pause, contemplate, value, and preserve what we have achieved. It crystallizes our flights of fancy into a store of myths and legends; it must be the source of religious beliefs, but also of dogma and prejudice. Having defied all laws, we often construct our own mental prison.

The last of the epochs of Paleolithic art, the so-called Magdalenian period, ends around 10,000 B.C. The works of the cave painters are followed by *pebble art,* small stones decorated in simple geometric designs, purpose unknown. One might be tempted to call it some form of Stone Age minimalism.

But another dawn was about to break. As the glaciers receded from the European continent, humans began to build permanent settlements, domesticate animals, and plant crops. Soon they were to discover metals. Around five thousand years ago they began to write. The rest is history.

Gene-Culture Dualism

The lives of all living things are shaped by two factors that have — since the first unicellular organisms appeared on earth — evolved together in a complex network of give-and-take: the genetic makeup the organisms inherited and the environment into which they are born. In this chapter we have described a third element, culture, that emerged with the first appearance of *Homo sapiens.* It followed the last known evolutionary changes in brain size. We have every reason to conclude that the capacity for, and the inclination toward, cultural innovation are biologically based; no species with a lesser brain has ever produced a culture.

Let us pause for a moment and make clear just what is new about this feature. Biologists have pointed out that novel behavior may appear in a population of animals in response to particular needs or opportunities offered by the environment. Such behavior is often copied, and may be passed on from generation to generation. As an example, a certain breed of chickadees in England learned to peck through the tops of milk bottles left on stoops in the morning. The habit soon became widespread.[24] In the last chapter I mentioned that, according to one interpretation, different colonies of wild chimpanzees may be said to have developed cultural differences. What we are talking about, strictly speaking, are adaptations that are transmitted, not through genes, but through some kind of communication between individuals.

They lack, however, the most essential attribute of human culture, which is its dynamic, cumulative nature. Human culture *evolves*. Every cultural event leaves a residue and is itself the product of a long line of antecedents. Already in some of its earliest forms, culture transcended its original role of merely facilitating man's struggle in the environment and became an end in itself. The cave paintings and sculptures of the Paleolithic Ice Age are witness to the often unpragmatic expressions found in human culture.

Cultural evolution is frequently likened to genetic evolution — both are processes of cumulative changes, guided to some extent, no doubt, by some principle of natural selection. But just how much selection dominates genetic evolution is a matter of dispute among evolutionary biologists. Its sway over cultural evolution is even more controversial.

Culture, we saw, came in as a third factor (after genes and environment) affecting the lives of individuals. However, culture itself wields such strong influence upon our environment that we normally consider just these two: genes and culture, *nature* and *nurture*.

I want to avoid saying that these factors determine our lives, since this is too easily mistaken to mean that events in our lives are ruled deterministically by one or the other, or by some combination of genes and environment.

The dualist aspect has sparked one of the classic controversies. Which of the two is stronger? Which accounts for more of what our lives turn out to be? What shapes our talents, our aspirations, our morals? We will discuss this seesaw controversy and its powerful political overtones in the next chapter.

As physicist, I cannot help being reminded of that classical dispute in physics over the apparently dual aspect of the nature of light. The argument goes back to the days of Isaac Newton, who saw light as a stream of particles. His contemporary, the Dutch physicist Christian Huygens, believed it to be a wave. For a while, the particle theory was accepted on the strength of Newton's enormous reputation. But soon evidence accumulated in support of the wave theory, and by the end of the nineteenth century no one doubted that this was the correct interpretation. The twentieth century brought the big surprise: light also has the attributes of particles. For that matter, such classical particles as electrons and protons, and, in principle, even grains of sand, now turned out also to have the properties of waves.

But how are we to explain this dual character? The particle-wave controversy had thus become the particle-wave paradox. Eventually, a totally new theory, quantum mechanics, showed that there was no contradiction in this duality. Particle and wave characteristics were complementary aspects belonging to the same physical reality.

Is the nature-nurture controversy to be similarly resolved by invoking a gene-culture dualism? This solution is advocated by a group calling themselves *sociobiologists*. Their position is attacked with considerable passion by some prominent evolutionary biologists, in one of the most volatile feuds that currently rock the scientific community.

CHAPTER IV

Beyond Evolution

ARE WE PROGRAMMED in our actions by the genes we inherit? Is the environment, in which we must include the culture we have created, a more powerful determinant of our behavior? Is it nature, or is it nurture? Is it neither, or is it both? Few supposedly scientific questions have aroused more passions or more acrimony among the disputants. Massive data and more massive arguments have been mobilized, but no convincing breakthrough has occurred in this scientific trench warfare.

But since we are trying to assess our ability to deal with a very precarious epoch in human history, it makes sense to ask where we should look for guidance and what, if anything, we can do about certain human tendencies that have corrupted our past and threaten to shorten our future. If we are programmed, can we change the program? Can we *will* an escape from the dictates of genes or environment, or is free will a delusion invented by automata to disguise their own clocklike progression?

Ancient Greek philosophers were solidly on the side of nature. Aristotle believed in native nobility and in the inherited destiny of a few to lead in all human affairs. He was in this respect a true follower of that other elitist, Plato, some of whose teachings anticipate later doctrines of eugenicists. It is interesting to speculate about to what extent Aristotle's conviction affected the boy he was tutoring, who was to become Alexander the Great. At any rate, Aristotle's ideas had made a lasting impact on Western thought. The belief in native — we would now say genetic — superiority has since been the cornerstone of feudal systems that confer aristocratic privileges upon a small portion of humanity and make peons of the rest of us.

The Seesaw Begins

The Renaissance opened some doors of opportunity to those not of noble birth, in the arts, in science, and in commerce, without, however, lessening the power and wealth of aristocracy or the burden of the common man.

The first serious challenge to the belief in inherited gifts came during the Glorious Revolution of 1688 in England, which established the constitutional monarchy that still exists today. The philosopher of that revolution was John Locke.[1] In his *Essay Concerning Human Understanding* he describes experience as the sole source of all knowledge. There is no innate wisdom. Each infant is born as an empty tablet (*tabula rasa*), on which the environment gradually makes its imprints. From this it was gathered that, at birth, all humans are identical, a notion hailed by Voltaire half a century later and taken up another half century after that in the American War of Independence and in the French Revolution.

But the lofty notions of freedom and brotherhood did not always translate easily into actions. Slavery continued in the United States long after the declaration that "all men are created equal." In Europe the nineteenth century was a period of the most vigorous expansion of colonial empires. Darwin's new theories seemed to call attention more to biological than to social factors in the formation of individual qualities, reinforcing among English gentlemen the conviction that they belonged to a superior stratum of a superior race.

One such person was Francis Galton, Darwin's cousin, who at the age of twenty-two inherited a small fortune, part of which he used to organize an expedition to southern Africa. There he pacified several fractious native tribes, mapped some hitherto unexplored regions, and studied the anatomy of Hottentot women. This earned him a fellowship in the Royal Geographical Society.

Upon returning to England, Galton divided his life between the pursuits of a gentleman and scientific interests. He was anything but frivolous in his work and tried to make up with mathematical rigor for what he lacked in formal training. Numbers fascinated him. He thought much about the newly discovered laws of statistics, especially the so-called normal distribution, according to which measurable quantities were scattered with predictable regularity about a central mean. He once demonstrated with a simple statistical argument the inefficacy of prayers: members of the British royal family, he pointed out, had normal life expectancies, even though they were the most prayed for.

For a while, Galton was drawn to the infant science of meteorology — he coined the term *anticyclone* for the clockwise rotation of air masses around a high pressure center — but eventually became absorbed in his study of heredity. In his most significant publication, *Hereditary Genius* (Galton, 1869), he presented data on thousands of individuals whose accomplishments ranged from statesmanship to science to oarsmanship to wrestling. From the statistics of family trends in all these endeavors, he concluded that most talents are genetically determined.

He was convinced that neither poverty nor racial disadvantages imposed by society could inhibit true genius, nor could a mediocre person be raised to excellence by society. Moral qualities, too, were innate, not conditioned by the environment, a sentiment expressed several generations earlier in Goethe's *Faust*. In the *Prologue in Heaven* the Devil makes a wager with God that he can change the essential goodness of the ambitious Doctor Faust and win his soul. But nature wins out over nurture, as God predicts: After a life of folly and vainglory spent in the company of the Devil himself, Faust — simply by asserting his nature — is saved.

Galton divided all humans into sixteen classes on the basis of intelligence and proposed that the quality of the human race be improved through selective breeding. He dedicated himself to this goal, which he called "eugenics," with a fervor that was almost religious. "The more suitable races or strains of blood," he insisted, must be given "a better chance of prevailing speedily over the less suitable." Of course, the less suitable ones should be treated "with all kindness, so long as they maintained celibacy."[2]

It is clear that, to Galton, the sixteen classifications were very unequally distributed among what were called the "races" of man. He rated blacks two categories below whites, but admitted that there was a substantial overlap. Blacks at the top of their distribution curve were more intelligent than the average white. As Richard Morris has pointed out, "the scientists of the Victorian age were blatant racists," and "scientific antiracism dates only from the end of World War II."[3] What is often overlooked is that in the then prevailing scientific dogma, women shared with the non-Aryan races their alleged moral and intellectual inferiority.

The categorization of groups on the basis of averages, real or imagined, is, of course, a typological approach, and is, in that sense, a throwback to pre-Darwinian thinking. But it was Darwin himself who proclaimed man to be superior to woman.

The Individual and the Group

The dilemma beween individual and group characteristics has vexed psychologists almost as much as the nature-nurture problem. We can formulate the question this way: To what extent are we justified in judging the individual on the basis of the average qualifications of the group to which he or she may legitimately be assigned?

Let us take a concrete example. You are director of admissions at a graduate school of a major university, and you are scanning applications coming from candidates with varying backgrounds. You look at the grades they earned as undergraduates, letters of recommendation, their GRE, MCAT, LSAT, or other test scores. Then there are the schools to consider. A B from Harvard counts more than an A from a college you never heard of. After adding all these items, a picture of the candidate forms in your mind. You will, finally, send the letter of acceptance (or rejection) without having seen the candidate or heard him or her speak.

Is this procedure fair? Is the Harvard graduate necessarily a better choice than the one from F. F. F. College? You have statistics to back up your decision. The Harvard graduates, taken as a group, have unquestionably a superior performance record. Of course, your choice of this particular Harvard graduate may turn out to be disappointing. But in your career as director of admissions you will have to make many such decisions, and there is no question that you will do well by consistently choosing Harvard over F.F.F. Your occasional dud from Harvard is part of the statistics and totally expected. The rare genius from old Triple F will never be missed, because he or she will never be known.

Similar arguments can be made about the predictive values of cumulative grade averages and other test scores. There is no question, therefore, that, from the point of view of the director of admissions, the above procedure seems justified. And it is just as clear that it is unsatisfactory from the point of view of the applicant who has little chance to explain any shortcomings, or express what he or she believes are qualifications to be considered.

We have invoked statistics to assign average performances to a large variety of groups, and derive from this expectation values for the success of individual members of these groups. The results are often summed up categorically: "Americans have more ingenuity." "Orientals are more industrious." "Latins make better lovers."

We realize that many of these assignments result from phony observations, shoddy or loaded statistics, uncritical reasoning, or prejudice. But let us look at the ones that seem statistically sound, like the future success rate of high achievers coming from Ivy League colleges. We cannot really fault the admissions director for this use of the only information available. But all too often these data are treated as though they were a complete description.

To point out the flaw in this argument, consider another hypothetical situation: I am advertising my services as a consultant on weather. As proof of my qualifications I cite my remarkable record of correctly predicting the next day's weather. I have achieved this record by following a simple formula, that of always announcing for tomorrow whatever the weather is today. If it rains today, I call for rain tomorrow. If it's sunny, I predict sun. My success stems from the fact that in most locations weather patterns persist over a number of days, so that my batting average may even exceed that of the U.S. Weather Bureau. Of course, my predictions are worthless. Even though statistically accurate, they lack what you really want from a meteorologist: the prediction of the unlikely events, the hurricanes, the blizzards, the sudden changes in temperature.

Predicting individual performance from group averages is not unlike predicting tomorrow's weather from today's. Jeremy Bernstein tells the story of how Julian Schwinger, one of the giants of modern physics, came to be admitted to Columbia University. He was at the point of flunking out of City College because of a dismal scholastic record, which included an F in English. One day I. I. Rabi, a Nobel laureate and professor of physics at Columbia, was discussing a new and challenging paper with one of his students, Lloyd Motz. It was by Einstein, Podolsky, and Rosen and explored what they believed to be the limitations of quantum mechanics. Young Schwinger walked in on their discussion. Bernstein quotes Rabi's story: "'So I told him to sit down someplace, and he sat down. Motz and I were arguing, and this kid pipes up and settles the argument. . . . And I said, "Who the hell is this?" . . . I talked with him for a while and was deeply impressed.'" When Rabi tried to get Schwinger admitted to Columbia on a scholarship, the director of admissions balked. A scholarship? He didn't even want to admit him. It took the combined efforts of three eminent physicists, I. I. Rabi, Hans Bethe, and George Uhlenbeck, to persuade the administration that in the case of Julian Schwinger the group characteristics were a poor match to the individual's worth.

The Eugenics Movement

Galton's doctrines of improving the human race by selective breeding fell on fertile ground, causing, by the end of the nineteenth century, a complete reversal both in England and in the United States of previously cherished notions of human equality at birth.

At the same time the teachings of the English philosopher Herbert Spencer became very popular, especially in the United States. It was he who first used the phrase "survival of the fittest," referring not so much to biological evolution as to the struggle of the individual for preeminence in the society. It was Spencer's belief that any attempt to assist the poor and disabled would only hamper the natural social evolution, since it favored the weak at the expense of the fittest. All social legislation was therefore *dysgenic*. This political philosophy, sometimes known as "social Darwinism," has since become a rallying point of the political right.

For a while, the eugenics movement took an unexpected turn to the left. In England, George Bernard Shaw, Havelock Ellis, and the statistician Karl Pearson combined socialist ideas with Galton's teachings. It was their view that class distinctions determined who should marry whom, much to the detriment of the human race. They argued that eugenic principles should be applied instead of class distinctions. Pearson also managed to attract members of the newly founded women's movement, among them Annie Besant and Olive Schreiner.

In science *biometry* became the new rage. Emulating the successful quantitative approach of the physical sciences, biometrists made every human quality the object of intensive quantification and statistical analysis. The end result was almost always the same: strong evidence was cited for a biological basis of both talents and deficiencies. Intelligence, musical talent, and leadership qualities were inherited, as were feeblemindedness, criminality, epilepsy, and tuberculosis, also "nomadism," shiftlessness, alcoholism, and "pauperism." In what was perhaps the kookiest misapplication of Mendelian genetics, the American eugenicist Charles Davenport coined the name *thalassophilia* for an affliction that drew men to the sea. It was clearly congenital, as evidenced by the high incidence of naval officers and seamen in some New England families. Davenport saw it therefore as resulting from a recessive gene that, like hemophilia, was expressed only in the male offspring, but was also carried by the female.

In the United States, largely through the work of Davenport and the influence of Herbert Spencer, the eugenics movement became increasingly conservative and engendered laissez faire capitalism rather than socialist ideas. Davenport, with the support of wealthy contributors, John D. Rockefeller, Jr., among them, founded the Eugenics Record Office at Cold Spring Harbor on Long Island, which functioned as the nerve center of the American eugenics movement. It had as its objective the collection of the most extensive family records from all over the United States, as well as the training of young men and women to carry out the necessary fieldwork and research in heredity.

On the basis of the "scientific" findings of the Record Office, American eugenicists lobbied for the kind of legislation they thought necessary for the improvement of the race. This called for government control in two areas: immigration and reproduction. With regard to the first, they persuaded Congress that America was in danger of having its population deteriorate as a result of the influx of "inferior" races. Increasing crime rates and overcrowded institutions for the mentally deficient were cited as evidence that such deterioration was already in progress.

Respected sociologists and psychologists made pronouncements on the "superiority of Nordics and the undesirable traits of Mediterranean peoples," who were "prone to feeblemindedness and crimes of sex and violence." When Calvin Coolidge was vice president, he echoed the "scientific" findings of the day with the statement that "America must be kept American. Biological laws show . . . that Nordics deteriorate when mixed with other races."[5] It was Coolidge, also, who later signed into law the Immigration Act of 1924, which severely restricted the flow of people from southern Europe. Oriental influx, already greatly reduced by previous legislation, was now effectively cut off.

The other concern of eugenicists was the "quality of the protoplasm" that was already within U. S. shores. By this they meant the totality of features they believed to be inscribed in the collective genes of the population. (It was not known at the time that this genetic material resided in the nuclei of cells in the form of a large molecule we call DNA.)

Since feeblemindedness and criminality were believed to be the results of defective genes, it followed that procreation had to be controlled. Laws of compulsive sterilization were enacted in many states, and some 50,000 operations performed, most of them without the victim's consent, many even without the victim's knowledge. Stephen J. Gould relates the case of Doris Buck, who was sterilized in 1928 for alleged feeblemindedness, but was told the operation was "for an appendix and rupture." Later she married and tried to conceive. Only after years of futile efforts and medical examinations was the truth discovered. According to Gould, there was no evidence that she was mentally deficient.[6] Forced sterilizations continued to be carried out in the state of Virginia as late as 1972.

Prominent among the dubious scientific underpinnings of the eugenics movement was the proposition that a person's diverse intellectual qualities, drives, talents, and ambitions were embodied in a single entity called "intelligence." It was further claimed that a simple number, the "intelligence quotient" (IQ), could be ascertained for every person with a brief, standardized test that would constitute a permanent ranking of that person's capabilities and worth to society.

IQ ratings have played a powerful role in American intellectual life. Eugenicists rejected any suggestion that environment could in any way affect these scores. The American biologist Frederick Adams Woods stated in 1910 that "experimentally and statistically, there is not a grain of proof that ordinary environment can alter the salient mental and moral traits in any measurable degree from what they were predetermined to be through innate influences."

The Seeds and Fruits of Racism

It was inevitable that comparative studies would soon be undertaken, in which the statistical distribution of IQ scores among different ethnic and racial groups were compared. The most sweeping of these was probably the study by the U.S. Army on 1,700,000 recruits during World War I.[7] The results led the American eugenicist Theodore Lothrup Stoddard (1923) to proclaim his "iron law of inequality," which contained these axioms: "1. that the old 'Native American' stock, favorably selected as it was from the races of northern Europe, is the most superior element in the American population; 2. that subsequent immigrants from northern Europe, though coming from substantially the same racial stocks, were less favorably selected, and averaged somewhat less superior; 3. that the more recent immigrants from southern and eastern Europe average decidedly inferior to the northern European elements; (4) that the negroes are inferior to all other elements."[8]

The old Lamarckian doctrine that characteristics acquired by a person during his or her lifetime can be passed on to future generations was, as Stoddard pointed out, a happy delusion. It would have provided a simple means for the improvement of the human race — the only means, since civilization advanced too fast for evolution to keep up. At the time when this doctrine was popular, pregnant women would immerse themselves in art and literature and think noble thoughts, convinced that this would enhance the nobility of their offspring.

When Darwinian biology rejected Lamarck, mankind was seen in a most precarious and alarming situation. According to Stoddard, civilizations die when the race is deprived of its superior element. The process has been repeated time and again: "Upon the successful superior, civilization laid both her highest gifts and her heaviest burdens. . . . Glowing with the fire of achievement, he advanced both himself and civilization. Absorbed in personal and social matters, racial matters were neglected. Late marriage, fewer children, and celibacy combined to thin the ranks of the successful, diminish the number of superior strains, and thus gradually impoverish the race." The end of civilization would come when "drained of its superiors, and saturated with dullards and degenerates, the stock could no longer support its civilization."

Stoddard's fears may seem outlandish, but they are only a cruder way of expressing a concern Darwin had voiced earlier. Alfred Russel Wallace tells us that "in one of my last conversations with Darwin he expresses himself very gloomily on the future of humanity, on the ground that in our modern civilization natural selection had no play, and the fittest did not survive. Those who succeeded in the race for wealth are by no means the best or the most intelligent, and it is notorious that our population is more largely renewed in each generation from the lower than from the middle and upper classes."[9]

Stoddard's contempt for all but the "successful superior" is expressed in another grim scenario. It is that of the "misguided superior," who, "capable of civilized success, but cast into the depths by social injustice or individual wrong-doing," becomes the champion of the "vast army of the unadaptable and the incapable," whom Stoddard simply calls the "Under Man." In an obvious reference to the Bolshevik revolution, he describes the inevitable fate of the misguided superior:

> Flattered by designing scoundrels, used to sanctify their sinister schemes, and pushed forward as a figurehead during the early stages of revolutionary agitation, the triumph of the revolution brings him to a tragic end. Horrified at the sight of barbarism's unmasked face, he tries to stay its destructive course. In vain! The Under Man turns upon his former champion with a snarl and tramples him into the mud.[10]

It was not uncommon for learned discussions to degenerate into pompous oratory as it did here. Note the implicit assumption that the less gifted are also morally corrupt. Stoddard coined a technical term to describe the Under Man's brutal revenge: he calls it the "atavistic revolt."

Mainline eugenicists were in the habit of stressing their scientific credentials and pointing out that their views merely reflected the best the new science of biology had to offer. They saw themselves as the intellectual heirs of Charles Darwin.

Eventually a break appeared between the partisans of eugenics and a large portion of the scientific community. Among the severest critics of eugenics were the British biologists J. B. S. Haldane and Julian Huxley and the American zoologist Herbert S. Jennings. The American geneticist Raymond Pearl called eugenics "a mingled mass of ill grounded and uncritical sociology, economics, anthropology, and politics, full of emotional appeal to class and race prejudices, solemnly put forth as science, and unfortunately accepted as such by the general public."[11]

The IQ test continued to be accepted as the one hard measurement of individual quality. But there were occasional doubters. The psychologist Otto Klineberg published in 1935 a critical study of so-called racial characteristics and IQ tests. Regarding the first topic, he came to the conclusion that there was no scientific basis for any hierarchic ranking of existing races, that, in fact, great confusion existed over what constituted a race. On the subject of the IQ, he pointed out that the standard tests are highly dependent on the cultural background of the subject. He cites as examples the children of Dakota Indians, who had been brought up to answer questions only when they were absolutely sure of the answer, and some Australian natives, who traditionally treated problems through community efforts. The Australians were puzzled when the examiner gave them "no assistance, even when, as with one tribe he was testing, he had just been made a tribal member."[12]

In the U.S. Army tests of 1917, which had shown such large disparities between different ethnic groups and led to the particularly low ranking of blacks, Klineberg pointed to statistics showing that northern blacks generally ranked higher than southern whites, a feature that has come to be known as the "Klineberg twist." As an example, the median scores of black recruits from New York, Illinois, and Ohio exceeded those of whites from Mississippi, Kentucky, Arkansas, and Georgia. At first, this was interpreted as being due to selective migration. The blacks who had migrated north were perhaps the more intelligent of the race. Klineberg, in two careful studies, showed that this was not a valid explanation. In the first, he examined the school records in Birmingham, Nashville, and Charleston of 500 black children who had subsequently migrated north. A comparison of their grades with those of children who had not migrated showed no statistically significant differences. If the school records were any indication, it did not appear that those who later went north were any more intelligent.

Even more telling was the second study, in which a variety of standard intelligence tests were given to 3,000 black school children in New York City. When the results were grouped according to the length of time the child had spent in New York, Klineberg found that the newly arrived had scores comparable to those of southern blacks, but that after one, two, and three years the scores had increased significantly.

Two conclusions must be drawn from these data. The IQ tests do not measure *native* intelligence, but something that depends strongly on the environment, and the hierarchic ranking of races according to intellectual characteristics is flawed.

German racism represents the tragic culmination of the doctrine of racial superiority. The myth of an "Aryan" race was invented by the nineteenth-century French nobleman Count Arthur Joseph de Gobineau (1816–1882). He asserted that all higher civilizations had sprung from that single strain of humans and will continue to do so. In the early thirties the Germans let themselves be persuaded by their leaders that they were the keepers of the Aryan heritage, that they were physically and morally superior to all other races, and hence were entitled to more than what their World War I peace treaty provided for them.

Hitler's appeals found a ready audience among the jobless, the confused intellectuals, the frustrated militarists, and a few industrialists with big plans. His early speeches were examples of masterful demagoguery. They, not his later ravings, should be studied carefully to make us aware of how vulnerable we can be to suggestions of wounded pride and the promise of greatness restored. The facile manipulation of crowds has always been a menace to civilized society. Beware of the orator!

The formula Hitler applied in these superbly staged rallies was very much like the one so successfully used by Urban II (see p. 12): pride, promissory glory, and a thoroughly dehumanized adversary. The villains this time were the foreign politicians who tried to hold Germany to the Versailles peace accord and, of course, the Jews. More and more it was "international Jewry" that was blamed for all of Germany's ills.

With the outbreak of World War II, the carefully nurtured hatred exploded in what was perhaps the millennium's blackest period: the systematic and cold-blooded slaughter of six million Jews — the Holocaust.

When the magnitude of the crime became apparent at the end of the war, the civilized world was stunned. The doctrine of eugenics and its racist derivatives, already challenged on scientific grounds, were held in low esteem by most of the intelligentsia, although racial practices continued to this day, and the full lesson of the Holocaust has yet to be learned.

The reaction against the supposedly all-powerful gene took many forms. A sharp distinction came to be made by many geneticists between physical characteristics, which are inherited, and mental characteristics, which were attributed to the environment. A kind of dogmatic egalitarianism replaced the earlier belief in the superiority of some races. In the United States, the civil rights movement of the sixties, further accelerated by the revulsion against the Vietnam War and what many saw as its racist overtones, was perhaps the high point of this new spirit of equality among the races.

Inevitably, the effects of the environment seemed to occupy a larger role in human affairs, and Freudian notions about early traumas and repressed memories enjoyed new popularity. Mental diseases were generally believed to be caused by excessive stress or unusual early experiences. Treatments, accordingly, were also mostly directed toward uncovering, discussing, and reliving the traumas. The behaviorist school of psychology, from J. B. Watson to B. F. Skinner, holds that all actions are traceable to environmental influences, and that any behavior can be achieved through proper conditioning.

Nature Reborn

Of course, not everyone took part in this postwar swing to nurture. The issues, after all, were political, and in politics few people are ever converted to the point of view of their adversaries. After almost 2,500 years of the debate, there is no sign that the issue is about to receive a cool-headed, rational evaluation.

Thus, when the rigged statistics of the English psychologist Sir Cyril Burt, purporting to prove the genetic basis of intelligence, were first exposed as fraudulent, H. J. Eysenck, another British psychologist and an admirer of Burt's, declared, "the whole affair is just a determined effort on the part of some very left-wing environmentalists determined to play a political game with scientific facts."[13] On the other hand, the American geneticist Richard C. Lewontin, an avowed Marxist, makes a direct connection between "the old biological determinism" and the "New Right" of Margaret Thatcher and Ronald Reagan and argues that "any understanding of the works of biological determinism must go back to the roots of the bourgeois society."[14]

It was, in fact, impossible to return to anything as dogmatic as John Locke's notion of a tabula rasa. The science of genetics was flourishing now and produced an irrepressible flood of new information. The formerly elusive genes, first introduced as "calculating units" in discussing theory of heredity, were found by biologists to be real bits of matter. In the fifties, when Watson and Crick succeeded in revealing the structure of the DNA molecule, the gene emerged as a small section of DNA, a sequence of typically a few hundred nucleotides. Molecular biology came to be viewed as *the* scientific foundation of biology and engendered a new confidence in a physicalist interpretation of life, especially the mechanisms of heredity. In rapid succession, hundreds of physical and a few mental deficiencies were found to be genetically influenced, if not genetically determined. Thus, in an almost paradoxical development, confidence in both environmental and genetic determinism appeared to be building simultaneously. Today, we are still in the throes of that great impasse, and, although both sides of the controversy have become more sophisticated, neither has become less passionate.

The simplistic doctrines of the early eugenicists had to be abandoned. When it was realized that most detrimental genes were recessive, hence did not "show" unless a person received one from each parent, and that most of us carry several types of recessive detrimentals, sterilization could no longer be seen as a way of improving the quality of the race.[15] Geneticists came to realize also that genetic purity is hardly a desirable goal. The African cheetah is so pure that skin grafts are said to be possible between any two individuals. Such lack of genetic diversity causes the species to be extremely vulnerable to slight changes in environmental conditions. As it is, DNA studies show a high degree of genetic homogeneity among humans, with only small differences distinguishing different ethnic groups. Success of the human race depends largely on individual, rather than group variations of gene characteristics. Instead of being concerned, as Darwin was, about the contribution of the "lower classes" to our gene pool, we should see this as a healthy sign.

"New eugenics" is the name for a movement that was supposed to perpetuate the old idea of improving the genetic characteristics of the human race, while remaining on a sound scientific foundation. There was understandable hesitation about returning to theories of racially differentiated genetic qualities. But concern increased over genetically transmitted diseases and over a possible rise in the "genetic load" of detrimental mutations due to worldwide rises in the levels of radioactivity and chemical mutants and the increased use of X rays as diagnostic tools. It also came to be recognized that some of the genetic diseases showed racial preferences (sickle cell anemia, Tay-Sachs disease), and that some clearly affected the mental capacity of the victim.

Along with the recognition of these problems came a rapidly growing capacity to forecast risks, to render early diagnoses, and, in some cases, to take corrective measures. Through the technique of amniocentesis it became possible to diagnose genetic defects in the fetus, providing the parent with the option to terminate pregnancy.

The gene for Huntington's chorea is dominant. This means that a person has a 50 percent chance of being stricken with it if either parent was a Huntington's victim. He or she may lead a normal, healthy life until about age forty, when the symptoms begin to appear. But now there exists a test for the genetic marker that can tell an individual many years in advance that he or she will eventually be faced with the severe symptoms of the disease. This may have a devastating effect on the mental state of the individual, and there will certainly be many who would rather not know. On the other hand, it is possible that, with future advances in medical science, he or she will be more likely to seek and receive effective relief. The progress of science brought with it the usual cultural fallout: widening knowledge, increased power, burgeoning ethical dilemmas. Our ability to think will always generate the need for further, more searching deliberation.

The search for genetic factors has now reached almost frantic proportions. Scarcely a week goes by without some new revelation about genetic links appearing in the scientific literature and from there spilling over into the popular news media. By now there are several thousand afflictions claimed to have a genetic base, or at least be affected by genetic biases. These include muscular dystrophy, Down's syndrome, Tay-Sachs disease, manic depression, Alzheimer's disease, schizophrenia, and fragile X syndrome, a newly recognized form of mental retardation. But some geneticists have gone much farther, attributing behavioral tendencies to genetic factors.

It has often been objected that genes contain codes for the structure of specific proteins, not for mental or behavioral characteristics. Such qualities as intelligence, courage, or artistic inclinations were believed to result largely from environmental influences, with perhaps some polygenic factors, meaning that many genes may contribute in complex ways to the making of a single personality trait. Against this view, some geneticists now cite evidence that behavioral tendencies also have demonstrable genetic bases. One study even attributes as broad a quality as "shyness" to a heritable deficiency of a single chemical, dopamine.[16]

This new drift away from nurture (and toward a politically conservative philosophy) was initiated in 1959 when the Harvard psychologist Arthur Jensen revived the doctrine of a strong genetic and racial bias in the distribution of IQ scores.[17] Later, James Q. Wilson and Richard Herrnstein (1986), also of Harvard, reported a study of criminal records of Danes who, as children, had been adopted. The study showed that the crime rate was highest among individuals whose natural parents had records of criminal convictions but was more weakly correlated with criminality among the adoptive parents. Wilson and Herrnstein conclude that criminality, like intelligence, is genetically determined. This was further supported by the strong correlation between crime and gender. Men commit between five and ten times as many crimes as women, and in violent crimes, blacks are five times as likely to be the offenders. Sex and race, both determined solely by genes, thus appeared firmly linked to behavior patterns.

The battle lines are again sharply drawn. The political right stands for genetic determinism, convinced that the laws of inheritance bestow upon some of us superior intelligence and moral rectitude and condemn others to mediocrity or worse. On the other side, liberals continue to emphasize the fundamental similarity of all humans and point to the powerful control exerted by the environment. It is in fact not difficult to show that the "compelling" statistics cited above in favor of the nature school may just as readily be explained as arising from environmental influences.

Just how slippery some of the arguments can be is shown in this example by Christopher Jencks in a critique of Wilson and Herrnstein's *Crime and Human Nature*.[18] The length of a person's hair, Jencks points out, is largely a behavioral feature (leaving aside baldness). Its strong correlation with gender could be taken as evidence for a genetically determined behavior. Of course, it is not the Y chromosome that compels men to cut their hair short, but rather a custom that fortuitously became associated with the Y chromosome. Similarly, Jencks does not deny the statistics cited by Wilson and Herrnstein that associate IQ and crime statistics with genetic factors but states that "heritability" cannot be established from these data. He is inclined, rather, to ascribe disparities in both intelligence and criminality to the complex ways in which genetic determinants (sex, skin color) interact with our culture to affect other behavioral factors. Blacks, for example, are more likely to be born into poverty, an association that has historical rather than genetic reasons, and poverty, in turn, may account for inferior education, lower IQ scores, and criminality. At the same time it is important to realize that the gene-behavior association, whatever its true nature, is generally weak and often broken by factors of clearly nongenetic nature. The incidence of murder seems to be affected more strongly by a host of environmental factors not all well understood. Murder is three times more prevalent in cities than in rural areas and five times more prevalent in the United States than in Australia, notwithstanding the fact that a significant portion of Australia's population is descendant from English convicts. Genetic predisposition toward crime — if there is such a thing — is here clearly overshadowed by mostly unknown but evidently nongenetic factors.

To confound the IQ controversy even further, James Flynn, a political scientist at the University of Otago, New Zealand, recently reported the results of examining IQ scores in fourteen economically advanced nations, using tests given to military recruits over periods of several decades.[19] His data show spectacular gains in the average scores, for which no plausible cause has been advanced. As an example, the average IQ of Dutch draftees has increased by twenty points in a thirty-year period. Of these, only three points can be ascribed to improved socioeconomic conditions. But the most startling aspect of Flynn's data is the fact that this remarkable rise in the population's test performance was not accompanied by any discernible rise in intellectual accomplishments. One measure of the latter, the number of patents granted in Holland in a comparable period, has actually decreased by one third. I offer a factor whose influence on IQ scores has, I believe, received insufficient attention. Performance on any test must be strongly affected by the testee's desire to do well. Perhaps the draftee of the seventies and eighties, more aware of the comfortable niches a modern army provided for the recruit certified "superior," simply tried harder. The same reasoning may go a long way, also, in explaining low IQ scores of economically deprived youths, among whom "intelligence" is not the goal most aspired to.

Culture on a Leash?

The post–World War II climate of weariness with doctrines of genetic determinism could not prevent the emergence of mounting evidence that there existed genetic links to many physical pathologies and some behavioral abnormalities. But a much more sweeping relationship between genes and behavior is envisioned in a discipline called *sociobiology,* or more specifically human sociobiology. It was introduced by Edward O. Wilson, a Harvard entomologist, in a sensational work entitled *Sociobiology: The New Synthesis.* The theory was later expanded by C. J. Lumsden and E. O. Wilson in their *Genes, Mind, and Culture.*[20] Here the authors define sociobiology as "the systematic study of the biological basis of all forms of social behavior." Thus, not just individual pathologies but the whole spectrum of human activity was seen as resulting from our genetic makeup. The choices we make in our everyday lives are, sociobiologists tell us, subject to strong biases imposed on our brain by the genes. The genes, in turn, are affected by culture, as Lumsden and Wilson see it. In a particular cultural setting certain traits prove advantageous, and the corresponding genes are selected in the evolutionary process, thus changing the composition of the gene pool. This cyclic interaction between genes and environment is called "gene-culture coevolution" or the "coevolutionary circuit" by Lumsden and Wilson.[21,22] In the authors' own words:

> Individuals whose choices favor their survival and repro-
> duction — and that of their kin — within the contemporary

culture transmit more genes to future generations, and as a consequence the population as a whole tends to shift toward the epigenetic rules and the forms of cognition and behavior favored by the rules. The coevolutionary circuit is thus completed: The epigenetic rules (or the genes, or the culture, depending on the starting point chosen) make themselves by creating effects that reverberate around the circuit, finally to be tested by natural selection with each passage through the life cycle.[22]

One might rashly suppose from this that genes and culture should be well matched one to the other, that the gene-culture coevolution would by now have produced the culture that is most conducive to our well-being and evolved the genetic makeup most compatible with our culture. S. J. Gould and R. Lewontin call this sort of reasoning the "Panglossian paradigm." (According to Dr. Pangloss, a simpleminded character in Voltaire's *Candide*, everything that happens is for the best.) The universe, especially the part that directly concerns mankind, is a thoroughly optimized system. Against this view, Gould and Lewontin point out that, contrary to Darwinian selective processes, it is possible for "human cultural practices . . . [to] drive toward extinction."[23]

It is difficult to reconcile Lumsden and Wilson's coevolution with the enormous disparity in the speed of cultural and evolutionary changes. We have already mentioned repeatedly that genetic evolution is much too slow a process to keep pace with our rapidly changing culture. Lumsden and Wilson realize this difficulty and they stress that significant genetic changes can take place "within as few as 50 generations, or on the order of 1,000 years in human history." They call this the "1,000-year rule." If we accept their estimate, then gene-culture coevolution may well have brought about such a happy balance back in the days of our hominid ancestors, when culture was relatively stationary over tens or even hundreds of millennia. By the time *Homo sapiens* arrived on the scene this relationship must have become strained already. It broke down altogether when the invention of writing accelerated the flow of human history.

At this point cultural evolution raced ahead because, as Gould explains in *The Mismeasure of Man*, "it operates, as biological evolution does not, in the 'Lamarckian' mode — by the inheritance of acquired characteristics." Also, "cultural evolution is not only rapid; it is also readily reversible because its products are not coded in our genes."[24]

But are cultural practices always readily reversible? They, in fact, often show great inertia to changes. Witness the persistence of religious practices, some of which span a significant portion of the known history of mankind. The same is true of political systems and of methods of carrying on and settling internal and international disputes. We are locked, also, to considerable extent into systems of practices in agriculture, architecture, and the pursuit and preservation of knowledge. It is this remarkable persistence of many of our cultural practices that makes it tempting, no doubt, to ascribe them to genetic determinants.

We have come upon an apparent contradiction here. I spoke of a "racing" cultural evolution and then of one that shows "great inertia." Both statements are true. The first reflects the profound changes brought about by science and technology and by such cultural by-products as overpopulation, depletion of resources, and general environmental deterioration. Paradoxically, our political systems are divided into monarchies and republics, democracies and dictatorships, as in ancient times; racial and ethnic rivalries seem to go on forever; and the ritualistic trappings in the worship of some deities have hardly changed in millennia.

But, even with these slow changes, the 1,000-year rule of Lumsden and Wilson seems hardly relevant today. The vitally important question is, as expressed by Howard E. Gruber of Rutgers University: "Can we as a species change our ways of thinking and acting more in the next 25 years than we did in the last 10,000?"[25] Gene-culture coevolution holds out no hope in this regard, and sociobiology leaves us at the mercy of genetic determinism, or, as Wilson puts it: "Genes have culture on a leash."

The elevation of the gene to its ultimate supremacy was completed by the sociobiologist Richard Dawkins. In his challenging *The Selfish Gene*, he proposes that our bodies are merely "robot vehicles" designed to perpetuate the "colony of genes." Our brains have no autonomy: "Genes are the primary policy makers, brains are the executors."[26]

These doctrines received sharp rejoinders from scientists who saw genetic determinism as a way of justifying the perpetuation of social injustices. In the eloquent refutation of sociobiology entitled *Not in Our Genes*, Lewontin, Rose, and Kamin write:

> ... biological determinism is then, a reductionist explana-
> tion of human life in which the arrows of causality run from

genes to humans and from humans to humanity. But it is more than mere explanation: It is politics. For if human social organization, including the inequalities of status, wealth and power, are a direct consequence of our biologies, then, except for some gigantic program of genetic engineering, no practice can make significant alteration of social structure or of the position of individuals or groups within it. What we are is natural and therefore fixed. We may struggle, pass laws, even make revolutions, but we do so in vain.[27]

But it is all too easy to slip from biological determinism into another type of reductionist explanation of human behavior: the proposition that, for better or worse, our individual lives are determined by the environment in which each of us happens to be immersed. As in so many other disputes, the political aspects of the issue — conservatives and biological determinism on one side, liberals and environmental determinism on the other — keep the discussion passionate and polarized.

CHAPTER V

Beyond Genes and Culture

To RECAPITULATE BRIEFLY, we have observed the fluctuating climate of opinion regarding the source of our behavior. We have seen the grandiose and pernicious tenets of the eugenics movement, with its dream of a "perfect man," fade in light of the realization that it would be suicidal to give up what little genetic diversity we have. At the same time it has become evident that a growing number of debilities and diseases, many with devastating consequences, have genetic bases, and that the "load" of detrimental genetic markers may be increasing as a result of new mutagenic effects in our environment.

Genetic control of behavior was suggested by studies on the incidence of criminality, and a broad theory of biological determinism, called *sociobiology*, was introduced by E. O. Wilson. This produced strong reactions from scientists with avowed liberal leanings. "Liberal ideology," says Lewontin, "has followed a cultural determinism, emphasizing circumstance and education, biological determinism locates such successes and failures of the will and character as coded, in large part in an individual's genes."[1]

Let us be clear about the unquestioned role of social advantages and disadvantages in the lives of all of us, just as genetic biases toward one or another behavior pattern can no longer be ignored. But that is different from saying that either genes or environment, or any simple combination of the two, allow us to draw firm conclusions about the course of any individual life.

The Gene-Culture Paradigm

Unfortunately, the word *determinism* means different things to different people. I take it that a set of factors determines the outcome of a process if to every set of such factors there corresponds a definite outcome, and if the same set would always lead to the same outcome. The term is also often taken to mean that it is in principle possible to predict what that outcome should be.

In fairness, it must be said that while neither side of the controversy defines *its* determinism quite as narrowly, each will frequently admit that other factors also enter into the equation. Thus, few advocates of cultural determinism would deny that genetic factors do play a role in shaping human behavior. But in the ensuing arguments both sides frequently portray the other as holding to the more rigid, doctrinaire interpretation.

Realizing this state of affairs, one might be tempted to seek a middle ground in which both genetic and cultural factors together conspire to shape our lives. The great dispute then collapses to one of degree, rather than of kind. We are creatures with certain capabilities and predilections (given by our genes), and our lives are further shaped by the events that happen to impinge on us from the day we are born. Such a view corresponds roughly to what is known as "neobehaviorism," which sees the human being, in the words of a critic of that school, as "a puppet controlled by genes and rewards."[2]

This gene-plus-culture, double-leash viewpoint is incomplete for two reasons and hence misleading. The first is a subtlety, but one of increasing significance. Genetic factors have a way of disappearing. Their recognition is often the beginning of their removal as determinants. The reason is that culture steps in and mitigates, and sometimes repairs, genetic impairments. We take for granted such devices as visual and hearing aids and all manner of devices and regulations to aid the handicapped. We dispose of a growing arsenal of drugs that can alter mental and physical disorders. Often knowledge is the only remedy needed: galactosemia is a genetically determined inability to metabolize galactose. It can have serious, sometimes fatal consequences. The mere recognition of this fact suggests a good solution: avoiding milk and milk products.

The new techniques of genetic engineering hold out the hope of direct repair of genetic damage. They are clear examples of how culture progressively usurps control previously held by genes. It would be overly optimistic to predict a golden age in which mankind was freed from all genetic strictures, but we cannot say of any one affliction that it is beyond human power of repair. So much for the "selfish gene"!

We now come to the second point that is, I believe, lacking in the compromise theory of gene-plus-culture determinism. It is the item so fervently rejected by behaviorists (neo- and paleo-), and generally played down by sociobiologists: the existence of an autonomous mind. I will try to make a case for it now and hope to strengthen it in the next chapter, which concerns the human brain.

The causal chain that leads from gene to behavior or from environment to behavior is sometimes clearly demonstrated: the mental limitations of the Down's victim or the malfunctions caused by severe environmental traumas, be they natural or inflicted by fellow humans ("brainwashing," torture, battle fatigue syndrome). But these are extremes. Most of our behavior cannot so easily be traced to its causes. We are, nevertheless, trying. We have a special *horror vacui* that impels us to bridge causal gaps with explanations that have a certain persuasive ring. We have amassed a veritable arsenal of such explanations to fit every taste: Freudian, Jungian, Marxist, Skinnerian. We may have a good theory about why John is a political liberal while Jane is conservative, and we generally overlook the fact that, armed with a knowledge of the same determinants in the case of Jack, we fail to predict *his* political leanings.

The difficulty of explaining, let alone predicting, behavior from genetic composition, the individual's "genotype," was pointed out by Owen J. Flanagan, a professor of philosophy at Wellesley College, in *The Science of the Mind.* "The road from genotype to a specific belief or behavior," says Flanagan, "may be much longer than Lumsden and Wilson typically map it to be." Add to this the effect of the myriad experiences gathered in a lifetime, and we are left with "a rule system of fantastically greater complexity than the one we are born with."[3]

Flanagan's description of the long causal chain between genes and behavior is, if anything, an understatement. To understand just how unrealistic are the assertions of either genetic or environmental determinism, I am going to digress briefly with a discussion of so-called chaotic behavior in physics.

Billiard Balls, Dice, and the Weather

The success of classical physics during the nineteenth century, especially the application of Newtonian mechanics to a wide variety of processes observed in nature, gave scientists confidence in a causal and orderly universe and in our power to follow its processes through established mathematical procedures. The most spectacular such applications occurred in the field of astrophysics. Here, the simple universal law of gravitation, together with Newton's laws of motion, enabled scientists to calculate precise orbits of planets and moons both for the remote past and far into the future. Such successes made us overconfident, and this overconfidence has spilled over from physics to other sciences, notably biology. Here it is frequently expressed as simple reductionism, that is, the faith that — given sufficient physical insight and computational power — all biological processes should become equally calculable and predictable. Physicists have long since learned better, but in other sciences this simple faith lives on.

The confusion occurred because for a long time physicists concentrated on "tractable" problems so frequently encountered in celestial mechanics.[4] But there are others. Consider the case of an idealized pool table: the felt offers no resistance to the rolling billiard balls, and the edges are perfectly elastic; a ball will rebound with exactly the same energy it had before impact. The billiard balls themselves are perfectly round and perfectly elastic also. Assume, to simplify matters further, that the table has no pockets and is located in a vacuum to eliminate all air resistance. In this idealized system, if one ball were given an initial kick, it would soon collide with others, and they in turn would bounce off the sides and make additional collisions. Since everything is perfectly elastic, no energy would be lost, and the billiard balls would continue to bounce around on the table forever.

Elastic collisions between point objects are rather primitive physical problems; any high school physics student should be able to solve them. The situation becomes more complex when we are dealing with extended objects. Spheres are the simplest, but now the trajectories of the colliding spheres depend critically not only on their velocities before impact but also on their rotational speeds and on whether they hit "head-on" or make more glancing collisions. Knowing all these parameters, the laws of physics again allow us to calculate the trajectories.

Let us go back to our idealized pool table now, and start with a precisely known initial state: the billiard balls are all at rest at known positions on the table, except for one that has received a kick and is moving in a known direction with known velocity. Soon the collisions will start. A physicist armed with a large computer could compute ahead, predicting future motions, and it would seem that we are again faced with a tractable problem.

Here we are quickly disappointed. Our precise knowledge of starting conditions might help us predict what will happen after one or two collisions. But soon we would have to know more. Because of the extreme sensitivity of the dynamics to minute changes in some of the parameters, we would soon have to take into account such "weak" effects as the rotation of the earth, stray electric fields, or tidal forces exerted by the gravitational pull of the moon. All this could in principle be measured and taken into account, but the circle of relevant factors increases spectacularly with each successive collision. It has been calculated that after fewer than ten collisions, an uncertainty in the position of a single atom at the edge of our galaxy, because of its gravitational pull, would make our predictions totally unreliable. The indomitable reductionist might object that "in principle" all this is knowable and perhaps calculable. The problem is, in fact, intractable in any sense of the word. Consider, for example, that the position of that distant atom itself depends, among many other things, on the positions of our billiard balls.

We can think of many such problems in which the laws of physics, though valid, cannot inform us of the outcome. The evolution of weather on a global scale is one such case. Meteorologists speak of the "butterfly effect": even with precise knowledge of all possible meteorological data at one time — surface and air temperatures everywhere, wind velocities, cloud distributions, ocean currents, industrial emissions, vegetation, glaciation — in short, all factors we associate with the dynamics of weather, and possessing a supercomputer that could relate all those factors, the beating of a single butterfly's wing somewhere would be sufficient to upset all long-range predictions.[5]

The rolling of a pair of dice is another example. Simple laws of mechanics hold at any instant, but the successive bounces constitute a series of knife-edge decisions so sensitive that the outcome depends on the minutest surface features, the feeblest gust of air, unknowable in their totality. In a grand conceptual leap the physicist declares the throw of dice to follow the laws of pure chance, even though strict laws of mechanics guide every instant of their motion.

These are examples in which a multitude of external factors make the problem extremely complex and untractable. There are other systems, containing what mathematicians call *strange attractors*,[6] which, without outside disturbances, have unpredictable dynamics, even though they follow simple deterministic laws of classical mechanics. One such example is the turbulent flow of a stream of water. These are called *chaotic systems*. The study of chaos is now an active area of research in mathematical physics.

I must emphasize that *chaos* here does not imply a total lack of order. The states accessible to the system are limited, and we generally know with what probabilities certain states can arise. But, knowing the present state with any conceivable degree of precision, we cannot predict with certainty how the system will evolve in the future. The mathematician David Ruelle, in describing the properties of simple equations exhibiting strange attractors, marveled that "Although the time evolution obeys strict deterministic laws, the system seems to behave *according to its own free will*" (my italics). This is certainly an odd thing for a mathematician to say about an equation. Later in the same article he tries to recall how he and his coauthor in an earlier paper created the term "strange attractor." He cannot explain it. "The creation of strange attractors," he concludes poetically, "thus seems surrounded by clouds and thunder. Anyway, the name is beautiful, and well-suited to these astonishing objects, of which we understand so little."[7] The situation is stated categorically, and more prosaically, by P. Cvitanovic in the introduction to *Universality in Chaos*, a collection of technical articles on the subject: "The often repeated statement that, given the initial conditions, we know what a deterministic system will do far into the future, is false."[8]

Out of the Green Hell

I have inserted the preceding discussion of pool tables, weather, dice, and chaos because I know of no better way to make clear our profound inability to follow the causal chains that govern our behavior. *Chains* is, in fact, a misnomer. It would be more correct to speak of a web of tightly interlaced and largely unknown causal factors. "With regular frequency," says the psychologist Michael S. Gazzaniga, known for his pioneering work with split-brain patients, "we find ourselves engaged in activities that seem to come out of nowhere."[9] The "nowhere" is of course the green hell of dimly perceived hopes, fears, desires, and aversions, of projections into the future, and of conflicting signals from past events so numerous and so faint that they elude our grasp and comprehension.

Is human behavior totally unpredictable, then? Not at all. Any chess player knows that if he puts his queen in front of the opponent's rook, the opponent will take it (unless he finds it advantageous not to). We often do predictable things, and it is a pejorative to say someone is as unpredictable as the weather. But the actions that can be predicted with near certainty are generally not the most interesting. As to the rest of our behavior, we can, for most of us, predict that it will fall within certain bounds of ethics and law. On the other hand, weather is not totally unpredictable either. It never snows in Rio, for example. What makes weather and, I believe, human behavior, chaotic is our inability to make long-range predictions with anything approaching certainty, even with perfect knowledge of all knowable facts. But it is precisely our long-range behavior — our choice of a career, our position on controversial issues, and all the difficult decisions that cause us to hesitate and ponder — that most affects our lives, and, through our many individual lives, affects the course of civilization.

If we are ever to relate this part of our behavior to anything, we must first acknowledge the existence of what I called the green hell of our motivational jungle, and deal with it as an entity that exhibits its own characteristics, not derivable from anything else, a *personality*, a *mind*. This is not too great a leap, considering that virtually autonomous behavior has to be attributed to much more primitive systems, the strange attractors.[6] We come to see "mind," then, as the third partner, the apex of the gene-mind-culture triangle, a new powerful agency with its own evolutionary laws, different from those of genetic and cultural evolution. The invention of mind as the rule system that lies between stimulus and action, more generally between the "is" and the "ought," is, after all, not so different from inventing "chance" to account for the tumbling of dice. And mind is strange in the same sense as Ruelle's mathematical attractors, that is to say, insufficiently understood and worthy of awe. But it is not strange in Descartes's sense of being apart from matter and independent of the brain. Thus, rather than subscribing to a mind-body dualism, I see mind physically based in the enormously complex network of billions of neurons, which reflects mankind's long evolutionary history and also contains all the images that have ever passed before our senses. We will take a closer look at this remarkable system in the next chapter. This physical basis, rather than limiting or demeaning the mind's capabilities, is the source of its incredibly rich dynamics.

There is a further aspect of mind that cannot be glossed over. Humans possess *consciousness*, which is another term we invented to cover another multitude of insufficiently understood phenomena. Whatever the source of this unique faculty, whatever brain mechanisms are responsible for it (we will look at some candidates in the next chapter), it provides us with the most powerful means of shaping our destiny. Erwin Schroedinger, the Austrian theoretical physicist who was one of the architects of quantum mechanics, in an essay called "Mind and Matter" calls consciousness "the tutor who supervises the education of the living substance."[10] It allows us to observe ourselves, to evaluate, to judge our predicaments, and to plan. This property of self-reference is the key to self-transcendence. It makes us contest and transcend our biological limitations and alter our environment "at will" to suit our needs and aspirations.[11] And, unlike the clouds and the billiard balls that must follow inexorably their hidden dynamics, we often catch a glimpse and focus the spotlight of our awareness on such feeble determinants as the beat of a butterfly's wing or the tug of a distant atom.

CHAPTER VI

Brain and Mind

THE POINT MADE in the last chapter was that the individual is more than the sum of genes and culture. The human mind may be constrained by outside forces or hobbled by its own inadequacy. But the prisoner thinks and plots — and dreams. At our best, rather than just drifting with the currents of culture, we are the creators of culture and will be — like it or not — the manipulators of our own genes.

The source of all this volition and ambition, the human brain, is not only the least understood, it is also the least accepted of our organs.[1] Few would dispute the role of the stomach, the liver, or the pancreas. But we often view the brain (the brain often views itself) with suspicion.

Ancient Notions

Some 2,300 years ago Aristotle believed that thoughts were made in the heart. We have known better for many centuries now, but the brain has never become a popular organ. To know something because it is somehow encoded in the network of neurons is thought to be a mechanical, an ethically neutral, kind of knowledge. But to know something "in your heart" is to *really* know it, and that knowledge has an aura of rectitude about it.

Telling a woman that you love her with all your brain would in most cases quickly terminate a romance. And even though that is precisely where all love resides, no brain-shaped golden amulets are exchanged between lovers.

We have never fully accepted the fact that this three pounds of tofu-like substance in our head is the source of all insight and all emotion about the world and about ourselves. More precisely, what sets us apart are the extra two pounds of brain matter we have gained since our australopithecine ancestors roamed the African savannah several million years ago, and even more specifically, the last pound acquired when the genus *Homo* spawned *Homo sapiens*.

Part of our reluctance to credit the brain with its prodigious wealth of faculties has undoubtedly to do with the fact that we just don't understand how it works — how it can possibly work. Unlike other organs, this colorless, seemingly inert, and structurally dull tissue didn't seem to *do* anything. Its apparent uselessness is further emphasized by the fact that it is not even protected by pain. It is the only organ on which radical surgery can be performed painlessly without anesthesia. No wonder that for a long time it was believed to be merely "unripe phlegm."

But the cavities in the brain, the so-called ventricles, the communicating chambers that are filled with cerebrospinal fluid that also runs down the length of the spinal column, caught the attention of early anatomists starting with the Greek physician Galen in the second century A.D. They became convinced that all meaningful activity in the brain resided in the dynamics of this mysterious fluid, or rather a mixture of fluids, the *humors.* As shown in the sixteenth-century drawing by Gregor Reisch, sensory information entered the first of the chambers and was carried through narrow passages into the other ventricles, where it was processed, stored, and eventually retrieved in some form. This hydrodynamic view of brain function persisted throughout the Middle Ages and into the Renaissance, and only the discovery of electrical activity in the brain about the middle of the nineteenth century changed that view. Today we know that this insignificant looking gray matter consists of billions of neurons interconnected through an exquisite network of trillions of fibers, and of

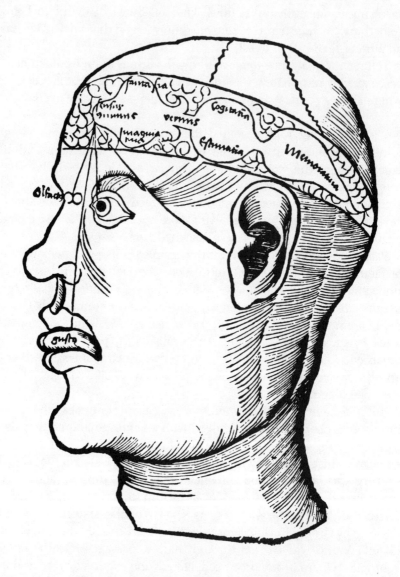

Brain functions according to Gregor Reisch (c. A.D. 1467–1525). This is an example of the cell theory according to which the prominent brain cavities, or ventricles, have specific cognitive functions. The senses of sight, hearing, smell, and taste are seen to converge on the first cell containing the sensus communis. (*In* Margarita Philosophica, *G. Reisch, Heidelberg, 1504*)

junctions, the *synapses,* numbering some hundreds of trillions. Somehow, this immensely complicated system receives, processes, expresses, and responds to everything that happens around us. By the end of the nineteenth century the ventricles and the cerebrospinal fluid were regarded as little more than an internal sewer system that carried away the brain's waste products.

It is interesting to note, though, that ancient notions, even if officially abandoned and discredited in one discipline, have a way of continuing in disguised form in another. No longer does anyone believe that sense impressions are carried into the inner chambers of the brain on waves of cerebrospinal fluid, there to be stored and brought up later as memories, emotions, or thoughts.[2] But the idea of some form of hydrodynamic mechanism is implicit in much of psychoanalytic doctrine, which lays great stress on the dangers of pressure building up in our psyche when painful memories are repressed. It is not evident that it is better to bring up, dredge up, and, if necessary, to vomit up nasty events from the past, rather than trying to forget them.[3] But Freud, in his theory of repression, treats past experiences as an incompressible fluid that can be pushed from one place in the brain to another but cannot be abolished. The repressed recollection must surface somewhere else with dire consequences. Such is the modern psychohydraulic version of Galen's old theory of humors.

On the other hand, modern brain research has become very sophisticated and has spawned an enormous outpouring of learned papers. Investigations are pushed in many directions by teams of physiologists, biochemists, biophysicists — even mathematicians, engineers, and computer experts — all united under the vast umbrella known as the Society for Neuroscience. But what have we really learned? Are we any closer to understanding the workings of the human mind?

The Elusive Mind

One trouble with brain research is that we really don't know what we are after. I don't mean that the neurologist who studies abnormalities — how to diagnose them and how to treat them — does not have well-defined and worthy aims. The same goes for the neurophysiologist, who tunes in to the neural blips that convey sensory messages, or traces the stream of motor commands from the peripheral motoneurons up the spinal chord to their sources in the neocortex. There, sensory neurophysiologists meet motor neurophysiologists, like two drilling teams coming together at the center of a newly completed tunnel.

But, having thus spanned the neural machinery from end to end, scientists are no closer to answering the most fundamental questions about the brain than they were a century ago: Is there a free will, and how do we explain it? Where is the seat of our feeling of selfhood? What is consciousness? What is mind?

Most scientists see it as a function — some call it an *epiphenomenon* — of the human brain. This object that constitutes matter at its highest form of complexity and organization, in ways not yet understood, is held reponsible for all phenomena we associate with mind. Not everyone agrees. The noted Princeton physicist Freeman Dyson believes in the primacy of mind, with life a secondary phenomenon that only serves to "give mind opportunities it wouldn't otherwise have."[4]

However, the only mind each of us knows intimately is the one residing in our own brain, and the only minds with which we can communicate — discounting tales about the spirit world — are the ones that rely on the powers of memory, reasoning, and means of communication that to the best of our knowledge only a living brain can provide. We look at the brain, then, for the foundations, the *embodiments,* of mind.

Our labors have not been in vain. We have come to regard the brain as a *sensory-motor* device that takes messages from the senses, processes them in some fashion, and makes appropriate decisions in the form of commands issued to the muscles. The great attractiveness of this view lies in the fact that the events at both ends of the causal chain are open to scrutiny, and we can study the relationship between the stimuli and the responses. A whole school of psychology is based on this so-called S-R approach. The intervening neural machinery is often treated as a "black box." Psychologists used to be interested only in what goes in and what comes out, while physiologists succeed now and then in shedding light on some of the neural processes going on inside the box.

A striking example of this paradigm of sensory messages being converted by the brain into motor commands is the tennis player. Stimuli, mostly visual, are arriving in rapid succession, calling for instant evaluation and prompt responses. The player's brain must direct the precisely coordinated activity of many muscles and must do it rapidly. The process is a steady flow of messages in and out of the system, with very little delay in between.

The power and the value of this sensory-motor approach to brain science cannot be overstated. It has the potential of revealing to us a large part of the functioning of our brain.

But stimuli and action do not always form as tight a chain as in the case of the tennis player. Often they appear quite unrelated. We doodle and we dawdle. Sometimes, one end of the chain is missing, as when we take in sensory messages but don't respond. We watch, we read, we listen to music or to a lecture, we contemplate a work of art. A stream of information pours in through the senses — and, to all appearances, vanishes. What is happening? Is the input irrelevant just because it does not trigger action?

The mirror image of this situation is equally puzzling: sometimes actions seem to flow from some inner wellspring and bear little relationship to whatever happens to come in through the senses. We talk, lecture, write, paint. And finally, to confound S-R psychology, we *think*. The total lack of activity *or* sensory input that often attends this state was strikingly portrayed in Rodin's masterpiece. No significant stimuli seem to be entering. The brooding figure is completely turned inward, performing no actions.

But with "nothing in and nothing out," the state of the thinker becomes inaccessible and even irrelevant to the traditional behaviorist. This school, started by the American psychologist J. B. Watson and represented today by B. F. Skinner, contends that only overt actions can be subjected to scientfic scrutiny and that concepts derived from introspection, such as *thought, consciousness, sensation,* may be fictitious and must at any rate be dismissed from the scientific vocabulary.[5]

Skinner is prepared to overlook even some overt actions when they conflict with the behaviorist premise that they should be traceable to overt causes. Disregarding the tantalizing uselessness of Paleolithic art, Skinner suggests that early man "did not look at pictures or listen to music . . . when he had nothing to do, if we may judge from related species, early man simply slept or did nothing."[6]

Unlike Skinner, I would conclude that we may *not* "judge from related species." The human brain has introduced into the terrestrial biosphere a totally new element, absent in the lives of all other species:

the power of introspection and self-reference. Socrates was among the first to recognize that it is a human quality and a human obligation to examine one's own life. We can trace the fruits of these self-examinations back into earliest human prehistory. Nothing is left un-examined, and we finally come to ponder the very process and the machinery of our self-examination, the brain.

The Elusive I

Of course, the brain is not all mind and consciousness and free will. It serves many so-called housekeeping functions of which we are gen-erally unaware. It oversees and regulates our vital hormonal balances, regulates body temperature, blood pressure, the action of the heart, digestion, respiration — in short — all of our vital functions. But, all of these could, in principle, be taken over by man-made devices. Elec-tronic pacemakers, artificial hearts, respirators, heart-lung machines are not perfect substitutes for the real things, but they can enable us to live, at least temporarily, without control of these functions by the brain.

This raises an intriguing question: If our organs can be replaced by artificial devices or someone else's body parts, and if control over the proper functioning of these organs can also be accomplished without the help of the brain — many *ifs*, but we will assume for argument's sake that the answers are all affirmative — where, then, is the *I* about which I am concerned and whose life *I* value?

We can now give an unequivocal answer to this. It is in the brain. If your brain is dead, *you* are dead. Your heart may be beating in your chest, a respirator can make sure that oxygen-rich blood reaches your tissues, your organs are alive. All but one. If your brain has ceased to function, you will have no sensation of pleasure or pain. No thought crosses your mind, no memories, no desires. The permanence of this condition is what is meant by death.

But let us not give up so readily. The brain is, after all, just another organ. We may in time find a way to replace it also. And, if all the replacements were to function (and look as good as the originals), would you then feel satisfied that it is *you* that is surviving?

The question is, I realize, nonsensical as posed: if *you* feel anything, then you have indeed survived. And you won't be dissatisfied if you are dead. We have to formulate the question of selfhood differently. It implies a more than superficial connection with the past, an intricate network of memories and associations that the environment has laid down on the *tabula rasa* of your genetically determined brain. I would be tempted to say that *you* survived only if you succeeded in taking with you a substantial part of that baggage. Even the amnesiac, who has lost a good part of his memories, will have retained much of what civilization has taught him. He knows the customs of his society, and he speaks and understands its language. If he doesn't, we may as well say that his old self has ceased to exist.

If the delicate web of memories and associations constitutes a necessary part of our selfhood, then we must conclude that that individual's brain — not someone else's — is a prerequisite to his survival.

In *Windows on the Mind* I compared the brain with the computer, and I pointed out that the latter is immortal (though given to obsolescence), because parts that cease to function can always be replaced by new, identical modules. The electronic "brain" has a fixed architecture and an absolutely rigid way of doing things. A given problem, presented with a given software, will always produce precisely the same answers. By contrast, there is no distinction in the brain between hardware and software. The structure itself is changing with every stimulus received. It evolves during your lifetime, adjusting the intricate network of neurons and their delicate connectivity in response to your particular experience and to suit your particular needs. This is the gist of *neural Darwinism,* a viewpoint put forth by Gerald Edelman, a neuroscientist at Rockefeller University.[8] Thus, your brain is not only unlike any other brain, but — like Heraclitus's river — it is never the same twice. This fact is the foundation, the requisite of human selfhood.

Cognition

The processes that mold the native brain into the unique self-referent structure that can look at itself and perceive its own identity are often referred to under the general heading of cognition. This used to be a controversial concept, long banned from scientific discourse by behavioral psychologists. It has lately been resurrected and has become the focus of much attention.

The term is derived from the Latin *cognoscere* (to get to know), which in turn comes from the Greek *gnosis* (the act of learning, also judgment). It denotes the acquisition and use of knowledge, beginning with the arrival of sensory messages in the brain, their classification according to previously established criteria of categorization, understanding of the context in which the stimuli appear, and the resolution of contextual inconsistencies and frustrations.

We illustrate some of the facts and problems involved here by taking a look at our dominant sense, vision, which has been studied more thoroughly than others.

The figure shown here is a schematic diagram of part of what is called the *visual pathway*. Here, the lens of the eye (*L*) forms an optical image of an object in nature, a tree in this case. The image appears upside down on the retina (*R*), where it is transformed, or *mapped* into a similar pattern of neural activity. From there about a million neural fibers, making up what is called the optic nerve, convey that message to the next way station, a group of neurons in the thalamus (*T*). (Another, older, visual pathway that bypasses the thalamus is not shown here.)

If we could view directly what goes on at that level, we would see a shimmering pattern of neural activity resembling in shape the tree we are looking at. This *neural image* of the tree now passes from the thalamus to the various visual areas in the neocortex, such as *V1*, *V2*, *V3*, and many others that have recently been identified. Each one of these seems to be specialized in extracting particular properties, or features, from the total message. Color information is sifted in some center, texture in another, motion, contours — and somewhere the verbal concept TREE may be formed.

This much of the description is generally agreed upon. It involves mapping and remapping of the sensory pattern, and the extraction of features by pattern recognition networks. Borrowing from the language of computer science, the whole operation is often called *sensory information processing*. This sounds substantial but contributes very little to our understanding of cognition. The adjective *parallel* is often added to indicate that much of this activity is going on simultaneously in different visual centers.

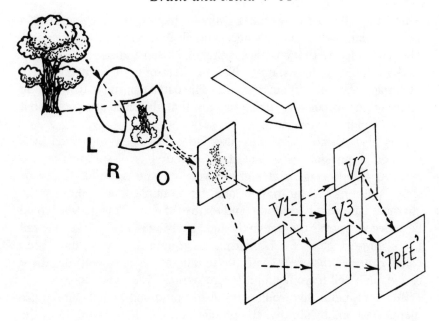

The classical conception of information flow in the visual system. A tree is imaged by the lens of the eye (L) onto the retina (R). From there the optic nerve (O) carries the information to a "relay station" in the thalamus (T), which passes it on to various areas in the neocortex (V1, V2, V3 . . .). Different features of the message are analyzed in different cortical areas, and somewhere the concept tree *is formed.*

Controversy arises over whether the processes described are sufficient to account for our perception of a tree in the visual field. Do the neural activities that appear at different cortical centers signaling color, contour, texture, etc., of a tree constitute cognition, that is, the conscious realization that what is before us is a tree?

At this point it is difficult to avoid the feeling that by the time the information has passed the first few stages in the neocortex, it has become too dispersed, since many centers know something about the object before us, but no center seems to have the whole picture. This is where metaphysics often takes over. Perhaps there is something, a *soul*, a *homunculus* that has access to all that scattered information. The naive picture that emerges is that of a disembodied self looking at banks of indicator lights, much like the operator in the control room of a complex plant or a nuclear reactor. The pattern of the many flashing lights somehow conveys to the operator that all is well or perhaps that No. 2 reactor is overheating.

It is also possible, and this alternative has been suggested by a number of physiologists, that the different bits of information are brought together again at higher levels and are there expressed by single neurons. There may be one, for example, that combines the characteristic shape, coloring, and texture of elms. This neuron would be active whenever the tree in the field of vision is an elm. We may call it an "elm-detector." Such neurons, assuming they exist, have been called *grandmother cells*, with the tongue-in-cheek notion that there is one such cell in your brain that recognizes your grandmother.

But homunculi, like souls, and even grandmother cells, only raise more questions by shifting the problem into another realm. Does the grandmother cell *know* what is out there? Does it *understand* something the lower neurons are not aware of? Or is it just another neuron, doing what neurons are supposed to do: send pulses to other neurons when its own input is large enough and otherwise keep quiet?

Instead of putting "a ghost in the machine," an expression coined by the British philosopher Gilbert Ryle, it is also suggested that the scattered bits of neural messages need not be brought together anywhere, but that the firing pattern of many, perhaps millions, of neurons is simply identical with the cognition of the source of all this activity. No unifying spirit or neuron is required. The shimmering pattern of neural activity is your cognition, thought, consciousness, and that is that. This view goes by the name psychoneural identity theory.

This approach has the virtue of simplicity. It also invites all sorts of speculation about machines that similarly process, analyze, and categorize visual information. Is this a form of cognition also? And can it be said, perhaps, that such a machine is *conscious* of the acquired knowledge? An advocate of what is known as *hard AI* (artificial intelligence) would say, "sure, why not?"

The question may be raised, why all this information processing has to be carried out in the first place. Isn't all pertinent information contained already in the activity of the million or so neurons in the retina?

The tragic case of Jonathan I. adds to the puzzle. The case was reported by the well-known neurologist Oliver Sacks.[9] Jonathan I., a painter who depicted the world in brilliant colors, became color-blind following an automobile accident. Unlike genetic color-blindness, which is a defect of one or more of the three visual pigments in the retina, Jonathan I.'s involved no damage to the eyes. Color information, along with other visual information, was evidently transmitted to the brain as before, but the world, including his own brilliantly colored paintings, now looked distressingly gray. It was, as he expressed it, "like living in a world molded in lead" and being surrounded with people who had "rat colored flesh."

Jonathan I.'s nightmare shows that sensory information alone does not constitute cognition. "Mr. I.," Sacks tells us, "could discriminate wavelengths as no retinally blind person could — but he could not go on from this to 'translate' the discriminated wavelengths into color, could not generate the cerebral or mental construct of color."

The damage to I.'s brain occurred, according to Sacks, at a relatively high cerebral region, a so-called association area of the cortex. I want to suggest that our perception of the color blue depends on having arrived at a concept of blueness as the sensation common to viewing the sky, irises, and bluebirds. This would seem to require the power of imagery, that is, the ability to fetch pictures out of memory and to view them almost as if they were real sensory stimuli. Thus, when we look at the sky, we can compare the sensation with the quality of sensation extracted from the recalled image of an iris. Without this imagery (constructed from memory), every sensation of color would be new, and no classifying concepts of colors, such as *blue* or *red*, could be formed.

A different cognitive function is our ability to synthesize images from partial or distorted sensory information. Humans excel in this faculty. In the Metropolitan Museum of Art in New York there is a canvas by the contemporary American painter Mark Tansey, entitled "The Innocent Eye Test." It depicts a cow that is being shown a life-sized painting of a cow. The animal stares at it passively and uncomprehendingly, while white-coated scientists armed with clipboards stand around assessing the situation. It appears that the cow's "innocent eye" fails to make the connection between the smears of pigment on a two-dimensional canvas and a live animal like herself. At the same time, what we perceive as the "live animal" in the painting is as flat and lifeless as the one in the frame within the frame. Our interpreting brain makes the distinction on the basis of a number of cues.

The phenomenon painted by Tansey is familiar to anyone who ever owned a pet. Most animals are notoriously unmoved by images of other animals, even when they appear moving in real color on a television screen. This fact may add a new dimension to our interpretation of Paleolithic art. I have in chapter 3 expressed my belief that the earliest pictorial representations were done for the sheer joy of discovery that lines and spots of pigment applied to a rock wall could evoke images of the real world. We take this evocative power of simple lines too much for granted. It does not surprise us when we see gargoyles in a cloud. This *eidetic discovery* is an expression of the enormous advance of the brain of *Homo sapiens* over that of his predecessors.

Sketchpad in the Head

Jacob Bronowski, in *The Ascent of Man*, commenting on Paleolithic cave art, writes that "the flat picture only means something to the eye because the mind fills it out with roundness and movement, a reality by inference, which is not actually seen but is imagined."[10]

The diagram on page 91 shows the classic picture of information flow in the brain from sensory receptors up the hierarchy of analyzing centers in the neocortex. We could have added to the right of the diagram a kind of mirror image, showing the convergence of neural commands coming down from the cortex and terminating on muscle fibers. This would have completed the diagram of the sensory-motor brain. The traffic of information is one-way in the sterotyped picture of the brain: up from sensors to the central nervous system, and from there down to the muscles. Muscular actions are reflexes in which a particular stimulus elicits a particular set of muscle twitches. Such reflexes may be innate and inevitable, such as the knee jerk, or learned, as the braking reflex in driving a car when an obstacle suddenly appears in your path.

Reflexes are generally fast. The complicated analysis of incoming stimuli, the choice of the appropriate response, and the organization of the entire muscular program are over in just a few tenths of a second. But the brain can also countermand. The American psychologist Michael Gazzaniga puts it this way: "The montage of conditioned responses that had governed biological creatures for all of time now dwelt in a brain system capable of thwarting their power."[11]

But a brain that can interdict the normal flow of learned information, the cortical reflexes, as they are called, must have as the basis of its decision making the power to conjure up alternative actions, envision and follow their consequences, and then make its choice. Such processes, call them thinking, involve the power of imagery. They are slow compared with reflexes, and probably of little use in a tennis game, but the added time buys an enormous adaptive advantage. *Homo erectus* must have possessed some of that faculty over a million years ago when he fashioned primitive tools, built fires, and devised new methods of hunting.

Ideas don't come full-blown, but as seeds that must be stored temporarily so they can be contemplated and developed further in what I want to call the *creative loop*. We increase enormously our power of reasoning by writing down our thoughts so that we can go over them, test them, rearrange them. The poet puts fragments of his creation on paper to feel its rhythm. The artist, before putting paint on the canvas, uses a sketchpad, and the composer tests his ideas on a piano. In all these processes the brain uses an external storage to stage its creation. We see the creative act as a bootstrap process in which a nascent idea is projected outward, to be materialized and reintroduced into the central nervous system through the senses.

But such external props only support and fortify the unique ability of the brain to fashion and hold images. In a theory I have developed in collaboration with some of my students at Syracuse University, the brain has its own built-in sketchpads, on which it can draw images that to varying degrees resemble those produced by real sensory inputs. This is like running the whole sensory process backward. The thought of a tree occurs at some high cerebral level, reaches out, and places the image of a tree somewhere into the visual pathway.[12]

In ordinary perception such feedback may just emphasize certain features of the scene before us and suppress others. Extreme forms of this process we call hallucinations. When we are in deep sleep, hallucinations come easily, because they don't have to compete with the images our senses report from the real world: we dream. But even in the normal course of dealing with the continuous stream of sensory stimuli impinging on our receptors, our perception of the world is punctuated by episodes of recollecting past events, guessing at the future, or just woolgathering.

In a reversal of the traditionally accepted flow of sensory information, the brain projects these images at some internal sketchpad, where they mix with the stimuli coming from the outside world. This is in conformance with the well-known fact — long glossed over by physiologists — that the traffic of information along most sensory pathways is not one-way. Peripheral sensory relays not only receive inputs from the receptors, they are also strongly affected by what goes on at higher cerebral levels. It thus appears that what the neocortex receives is not the unvarnished truth about the physical world outside; it is colored to varying degree by the brain's own expectations and ruminations. The sensory way stations preceding the cortex are thus seen as places where sensory facts are in competition with cortical fancy.

In the picture I have presented here, the phenomenon of *mind* arises from the creative loop, in which fragmentary ideas are projected peripherally, there to be viewed by higher levels of the central nervous system, which then again acts on the images. Norbert Wiener, the late MIT mathematician and founder of the discipline of cybernetics, talked about a phenomenon he called *circular causality,* in which an event A that causes an event B is, in turn, affected by B. In such processes the neat sequence of cause and effect may disappear. Time drops out of the process, and we are left with A being the result of A. An event gives birth to itself.[13] In the brain, such bootstrap processes can lead from the faintest, the sketchiest of notions, to elaborate and profound ideas.

The range of human activities that are rooted in such cyclic, or bootstrap, processes, is vast. Toolmaking could not have come about without them, and we have seen that the talent that allows us to associate two-dimensional lines and smears of pigments with objects in the real world requires more than the one-way sensory traffic of mapping and feature extraction. Falling in love, as only humans can, almost never "occurs at first sight," but gradually the image of our love object is transformed, and we are enchanted by our own mental constructs. This is also how we become enamored of political doctrines and philosophical ideas, and how we are persuaded that our country is always right, our religion the best, and our ethnic extraction superior to all others. Finally, our curiosity about the world around us is nurtured and kept alive by the exclusively human ability to follow questions with tentative answers that we can string together into coherent structures and modify according to fact or reason or fancy. The creative loop in our heads becomes the source of our art, our religions, and our science.

CHAPTER VII

Magic and Science

The Story of Two Bridges

I TRUST THAT we have by now firmly anchored the human mind in the brain and that we have come to see the human brain as a spectacular evolutionary triumph that has conferred on humans adaptive advantages that have made them undisputed masters of the terrestrial biosphere.

I have tried to show how mind may have arisen from a cerebral mechanism that allows us to create mental images that we can contemplate and elaborate in a cyclic action we called the *creative loop*. We see a distinct deficiency in this ability in animals. The dog whose leash is wound around a post in one direction is unable to visualize the simple solution of walking around the post in the opposite direction. Out of the creative loop has come our ability to make tools, to build fires, plant seeds, and domesticate animals.

But mind is not all adaptation, like the opposable thumb of apes and humans. It is rather, as I pointed out at the end of the last chapter, an innovation that has also brought forth a bewildering variety of unpredictable and often quaint behavior. Not all of it is related to survival. As prominent as his acquisition of practical skills and knowledge are man's apparent need for artistic expression, his awe and curiosity about the world around him, and his dedication to causes. The nonadaptive aspects of mind all but overshadow the evolutionary advantages, making mind appear a capricious biological extravaganza and sometimes a fatal flaw.

Throughout this book I try to stress that we are not drifting helplessly down an evolutionary stream, but that we have the freedom of self-analysis and self-determination. Once it emerged in prehistoric times as the result of evolutionary changes, mind has preempted evolution and is now the sole resource in our struggle for survival. It serves both long- and short-range goals. It performs superbly in solving the practical problems of our day-to-day existence. Beyond these, it has erected the magnificent structures that form our culture. These will ultimately determine the longevity of our civilization and perhaps of our race. We must examine them carefully for hidden flaws. To this end let us look at two of the most prominent structures conceived by the human mind.

The seventeenth-century philosopher-scientist René Descartes drew a sharp distinction between the mind (*res cogitans*) and the rest of the world (*res externa*). The gap between the two has come to be known as the Cartesian cut. While each of us easily identifies with the first, we have sharply divided opinions and attitudes concerning the second, which each of us faces across his or her own private gap.

The two endeavors that make up the title of this chapter are attempts to bridge the gap, to mend the Cartesian cut. Together with art, which is another, these activities have occupied a disproportionate fraction of human efforts, both material and spiritual. What is the fascination? Where do they lead us?

Let us take magic first. I see it as a search for power, or for *a* power, of a kind that is incomprehensible through rational analysis. It is *supernatural* power. In its narrower sense it is a reaching for individual power, a search for the *arcanum*, power exercised, or pretended to be possessed, by a few extraordinary humans, the sorcerers, the shamans. In the wider sense in which I would like to use the term, *magic* would also include the referral of supernatural powers to nonhumans, inanimate objects or animals, such as the gods of ancient Egypt, or humanlike deities like those of ancient Greece or the Judeo-Christian God.[1]

The classification of religions along with the more "primitive" cults and practices of magic will probably encounter some objections. However, I merely wish to distinguish as a group of world models all those in which supernatural powers play a significant role.

The bridge built by science is both more tentative and more ambitious than that of magic. Where the mystic likes to speak of "eternal truths," the scientist is content with theories. I will say more later about the nature of theories and the popular misconceptions surrounding them. The ambition that is unique to the scientific enterprise, and that has been the chief incentive from the start, is to arrive at an intellectual satisfaction we call *understanding*. This dream was eloquently expressed by the man who twenty-four centuries ago concluded that the world was made up of atoms. Democritus, in one of the few fragments of his writings that are still preserved, said, "I would rather discover a single causal relationship than be King of Persia."

But what is understanding? If science contains elements of art, as some scientists claim, one of these is the art of asking the right questions. I. I. Rabi, the Nobel-winning physicist, attributed his scientific curiosity to his mother. When he was a boy and came home from school she didn't ask him what he had learned, but would say, "Izzy, have you asked any good questions today?"

What then is a good question? To a scientist it is one that suggests, however vaguely, how an answer might be sought. And a satisfactory answer is one that reflects the path taken to ascertain it. "Is there life after death?" would not be a good question. But "How are atoms formed?" is now a good question, and the answer, that they are made in the hot cores of stars, spelling out the whole chain of causal relationships as we know them now, would have delighted Democritus.

Art is perhaps the strangest expression of the human mind. Far older than science, which had to wait for the written word, art has been with us for several tens of millennia. But we still fail in attempts to define it. While magic and science in their own ways are searches for truth (as well as for power), truth has little meaning in an activity that creates its own realities. Where magic and science are speculative, interpretive, and theoretical, art is creative. And, while magic and science define two poles in our approach to a world view, art does not stand long with one side or the other. Some see it as closer to magic. "The artist and the priest," says Denis Donoghue, "know that there are mysteries beyond anything that can be done with words, sounds, or forms."[2] But sometimes, artists go out of their way to shun mystery and seek realism in science. In its ideal form art is unimpeachable and incorruptible. While science and mysticism play out their spirited dialogue, art is almost like the solemn chorus in a classical Greek tragedy. It exerts, as Donoghue also states, "an interrogative pressure on those who see it (read it; hear it). . . ." Whether or not that is its objective, it provides a running commentary on the human drama.

Plato's Legacy

The tradition of magic owes much of its strength and longevity to one philosopher, Plato. In a new study entitled *The Trial of Socrates*, I. F. Stone speaks of Plato's "mystical raptures and engaging absurdities," which he compares to "gargoyles grimacing at us from the dark corners of a vast medieval cathedral."[3] Indeed, Plato's philosophy has all the trappings of what later became the Neoplatonist school of the occult, including the doctrine that true knowledge is for a select few. It must remain hidden from the masses, who could not understand it and would only debase it. Knowledge is *secret* knowledge. It is also a form of madness, *holy* madness, because it comes from the gods.

Perhaps the boldest contemporary expression of this philosophy was presented in 1960 at a Phi Beta Kappa oration given to the Columbia University chapter by the classicist Norman O. Brown. Here Dr. Brown states that

> mysteries are unpublishable because only some can see them, not all. Mysteries are intrinsically esoteric, and as such an offense to democracy; is not publicity a democratic principle? Publication makes it republican — a thing of the people. The pristine academies were esoteric and aristocratic, self-consciously separate from the profane vulgar. Democratic resentment denies that there can be anything that can't be seen by everybody; in the democratic academy truth is subject to public verification; truth is what any fool can see. This is what is meant by the so-called scientific method; so-called science is the attempt to democratize knowledge — the attempt to substitute method for insight, mediocrity for genius, by getting a standard operating procedure.[4]

Rarely has the adjective "democratic" been used in such a pejorative sense. Rarely, that is, since Plato, who despised democracy. I. F. Stone quotes from Plato's *Republic,* in which he suggests — or rather has Socrates suggest — that "the speediest and easiest way" to create the ideal city is to exile "all inhabitants above the age of ten, and leave the children to be re-molded by the philosophers."[5] And Will Durant, paraphrasing a passage in Plato's *Laws,* writes:

> . . . there must be complete state control of education, publication, and other means of forming public opinion and personal character. . . . Authority will replace liberty in education. . . . Literature, science, and the arts are to be under censorship; they will be forbidden to express ideas which the councilors consider hurtful to public morals and piety . . . the state shall determine what gods are to be worshipped, and how, and when. Any citizen who questions this state religion is to be imprisoned; if he persists he is to be killed.[6]

This is not an ancient version of Orwell's *1984,* but Plato's prescription for a utopian community. Most of us will find these statements shocking. Yet Plato has remained to this day somewhat of a philosopher's philosopher. The accusations leveled against Plato's teacher Socrates, that he was corrupting Athenian youth, seem less absurd when we consider that just a few years before his trial several of Socrates' disciples were prominent leaders in the bloody uprising that temporarily toppled democracy in Athens.

Magic and elitism went hand in hand in Plato's philosophy. One may argue that religion, too, is a form of elitism, since it graces only true believers. Faith is neither willed nor bought. It comes naturally to some of us. To others it descends suddenly at some turn in life, and to some of us it never comes. By contrast, *scientific* truth is what — in N. O. Brown's words — "any fool can see."

I have dwelt on Plato not because he was the originator of magic (he was not), but because he has been its most influential advocate. Much of occult lore predates Plato, and some of it was invented after him. Magic teachings originated in ancient Persia, Egypt, and India, and in the Hebrew cabala of the Middle Ages. Plato's name remained associated with magic well into the Renaissance through the occult teachings known as Neoplatonism. The secret knowledge included alchemy, astrology, necromancy, and other magic practices. Platonic mysticism found its way into early Christian doctrines through the writings of St. Augustine, who was an admirer of Plato.

Today magic survives in many forms, in the major religions, in cults, in so-called superstitions, and in such quasi-scientific endeavors as parapsychology. Tales of magic have enriched our fantasies, seduced our imagination, and appealed to our sense of wonder. They are ingested hungrily by the human mind — one might conclude that they contain some vital nutrient.

The endurance of magic practices and beliefs across time and across so many different civilizations suggests that it must serve deep-seated needs. Power, at least the illusion of power, is certainly one of them. Knowledge, or the illusion of knowledge, is another. The exploratory mind touches on many things and wants answers. Unanswered questions are like open wounds. They demand our attention. A myth or a magic explanation is like a balm, a dressing that allows us to attend to other things.

Astrology is a case in point. Events on earth are messy, chaotic, unpredictable. By contrast, stars and planets seemed to move in perfect, unalterable orbits. The ancient Greeks saw eternal perfection in the heavens, a notion that later found its way into Christian dogma. By being tied to the stars, the seemingly capricious earthly events were made to acquire an aura of lawfulness and direction. Astrology was therefore an attempt to make a *science* of terrestrial happenings, where otherwise there would only be confusion and uncertainty.[7]

Magic also appeals to our esthetic sense. Magic and beauty can be very close. Even to a nonbeliever a religious ceremony is often a thing of beauty. Religious fervor translates readily into inspired works of art or music. Finally, at their best, religions have instilled in us powerful notions of right and wrong and of compassion for fellow humans.

But many of the benefits derived from magic, the comfort, the guidance, the ethical mandates, come to us only if we accept the associated belief system. And if we question the truth of the assertions, we must be prepared to do without these benefits. Is truth that important? Are we risking chaos and anarchy if we challenge the foundations of religion?

But magic has also had its darker side. Religion has often divided mankind, sometimes with tragic consequences. In the antidemocratic tradition of Plato, there is often a strong tendency to legislate belief, censor expression, and control education. In America much of this revolves around the theory of evolution, the bête noire of religious fundamentalists. Watchdog groups such as Phyllis Schlafly's Eagle Forum, the National Association of Christian Educators, or Faith America have sharply increased the scope of their activities in the eighties. A study by a group called People for the American Way, reporting on the rising censorship in American education, reveals that half of all biology texts treat evolution inadequately, one-sixth fail to mention it altogether. Senator Orrin G. Hatch (R-Utah) attached an amendment to the Education for Economic Security Act in 1984, which would prohibit the use of certain federal funds for "any course of instruction the substance of which is secular humanism." In Louisiana references to dinosaurs were censored because they supported the theory of evolution, and a school board in Florence, South Carolina, voted to remove the *Merriam Webster College Dictionary* from the school libraries because it found the definition of certain words objectionable.[8]

But these are relatively mild examples of repression. On a global scale the manifestations of doctrinaire mysticism are truly frightening; witness the total loss of individual freedom and the mindless frenzy of Shiite fanaticism in Iran. This is an extreme example. But primitive magic practices, often embedded in fundamentalist religious systems, are on the rise elsewhere. They contribute greatly to religious and ethnic tensions in the Middle East, where territories are claimed on the basis of ancient religious tracts, and holy wars are proclaimed in response.

Still, mysticism makes good copy. Time-Life Books, a publisher known for its distinguished series of popular books on scientific topics, is now advertising the first volume of a new series called *Mysteries of the Unknown,* which, it promises, "will update your knowledge of clairvoyance, telepathy, and retrocognition," and make you "enjoy gripping tales of contact with 'the other side'."

Science

The doctrines of magic may seem irrational and antiintellectual, but the borders between science and magic are often blurred. The practice of systematic observation, experimentation, and rational deduction grew out of the Neoplatonist school of alchemy. As late as the early eighteenth century, Isaac Newton, who almost singlehandedly founded the science of mechanics, discovered the law of universal gravitation, and developed a form of infinitesimal calculus, was also a devoted disciple of Neoplatonism and the author of voluminous writings on alchemy.

The beginning of the break between science and magic is generally associated with that sixteenth-century maverick, the itinerant alchemist-physician Theophrastus Bombastus Paracelsus, who, in his ten books called the *Archidoxies,* lambasted his contemporary physicians as ignorant money-grabbing fools. He was the first to use, apparently with success, mercury compounds in place of the more accepted organic pharmacopœia that included cowdung among the more palatable products. He preached cleanliness in the treatment of wounds and was not afraid to attack religious fundamentalism where it interfered with what he saw as the true "Mysteries of Nature." This passage from the prologue to the *Archidoxies* seems to be aimed at some of our contemporaries:

> Nor do we care much for the vain talk of those who say more about God than He has revealed to them, and pretend to understand Him so thoroughly as if they had been in his councels; in the meantime abusing us and depreciating the mysteries of Nature and of philosophy, about all of which they are utterly ignorant. The dishonest cry of these men is their principal knowledge, whereby they give themselves out to be those on whom our faith depends, and without whom heaven and earth would perish.

He then defines his aim and method:

> But since this [God's] word is not exactly known to us, can only be apprehended by faith, and is founded on no human reason, however specious, let us rather cast off this yoke, and investigate the mysteries of Nature, the end whereof approves the foundation of truth. . . . From the aforesaid foundation we have drawn our medicine by experiment, wherein it is made clear to the eye that things are so.

The collection of works from which I took these passages is called the *Hermetic and Alchemical Writings.*[9] Paracelsus the scientist is also still thoroughly the mystic. At the end of the prologue he announces that the first nine of the ten books of the Archidoxies will be written in a form comprehensible to his disciples, but not necessarily to the general public "for whom we do not wish to make matters too clear." The tenth, containing the most sensitive truths, he may in the end decide to withhold altogether, to be "safeguarded from those idiots who are enemies of all true arts." In a final note he adds:

> And let no one wonder at the school of our learning. Though it be contrary to the courses and methods of the ancients, still it is firmly based on experience, which is mistress of all things, and by which all arts should be proved.[10]

Nothing in science can approach the secure knowledge of those who have faith in things supernatural. Theory is the closest scientists ever come to knowing something, and they are often chided that this or that pronouncement of science is "only a theory." This complaint is most often applied by Creationists to the theory of evolution.

To understand science we must first understand the significance of a scientific theory. This is a topic that has a long history and about which there has been much misunderstanding. What do we call a theory, and what function does it serve?

In the year 1610 Galileo Galilei published his first major work, entitled *Messenger from the Stars,* in which he presented astronomical data gathered with the then newly invented telescope. He made a strong case for the heliocentric theory of Copernicus.

In the old system that goes back to Aristotle and was adopted as dogma by the medieval Church, the earth stood still in the center of the universe. All around it the heavenly bodies, moon, planets, sun, and the stars, were objects of divine perfection: flawless spheres moving in perfect circles. The moon may appear spotted to the earthly observer, but such imperfections were only appearance, "marks of Cain" that had to do more with the imperfect vision of humans looking up from a very imperfect earth. The true moon was likened by Dante in his *Divine Comedy* to an "eternal pearl," into whose radiance he and Beatrice were received on the first stage of their celestial voyage "as water receives a ray of light."

Compared with Dante's poetic vision, the moon that appeared to Galileo through his telescope was a bleak landscape, scarred by ridges and pockmarked by craters. This was not the heavenly body the Church claimed it to be. When Galileo also saw satellites around Jupiter, phases on the planet Venus, and spots on the sun, he knew that he lived in a universe that Copernicus had envisioned sixty-seven years earlier, one in which the sun occupied the central position around which the earth revolved along with the moon and the other planets.

In 1616 the Church issued Galileo a warning. The exact form of this decree is in dispute, but Galileo was apparently told that the assertion of a moving earth was contrary to scripture, hence heretical. A distinction was made between stating such a view as a fact or just a theory. The latter was tolerated by the Church as an intellectual exercise. It was acceptable to proffer a theory about a moving earth, as long as you made clear that you believed in the fact of one that stood immobile in the center of the universe.

In his next work, the celebrated *Dialogue on the Great World Systems,* which he published in 1630, Galileo was reasonably careful to maintain that distinction. But the force and clarity of his arguments left little doubt about where he stood: the earth was a planet. The earth moved.

The Inquisition soon pronounced Galileo to be "vehemently suspected of heresy." His crime was that he went beyond theorizing and treated the heliocentric picture as a fact.

In a dramatic session the seventy-year-old Galileo was made to kneel before the assembled members of the tribunal, and — under threat of torture — forced to recant: "I abjure, curse, and detest the aforesaid errors and heresies. . . ." He is sometimes credited with a defiant *eppur si muove* ("and yet it does move"), muttered under his breath. But this may be fiction.

The role of theory in science has since then undergone a profound transformation. No longer an intellectual game or an uncertain groping for truth, theory is now the end result of scientific reasoning. Observation comes first, facts are carefully culled from controlled observations, sorted, and tested against one another before a successful theory can emerge.

The transition from bare facts to theory is a creative act, in which the human intellect constructs a quasi reality that is suggested but rarely demanded by the facts. To test the theory, the scientist then subjects this quasi reality to thought experiments. If the outcome agrees with similar observations in the real world, the theory is supported by these observations.

An example will illustrate: the theory of a stationary sun and moving earth was a bold and revolutionary assumption on the part of

Copernicus. It was a creative act that could not have been derived from facts available then by any kind of logic. Galileo now asked how in this hypothetical structure the planet Venus would appear to us from different positions in its orbit. He concluded that it should have phases like the moon, which is what he saw through his telescope.

Theory thus transcends fact. It leaps across the Cartesian cut. Facts alone are dull. But they stimulate us to speculate on the how and why, to search for the "causal relationships." When we do this, we are not only trusting our senses, we also show confidence in our ability to reason. We are on the way toward a theory. The intellectual satisfaction derived from this process — we call it understanding — is one of the rewards for having theorized. A good theory is thus the ultimate aim of scientific labor. There is no such thing as "just a theory."

This is not to say that a theory is forever. Better theories emerge as more facts become known, or smarter theorists are born. But a good theory is the very best we can get at any stage of a science. The great scientist-mathematician Henri Poincaré expressed it well: "Science is built of facts as a house is built of stones; but an accumulation of facts is no more a science than a heap of stones is a house."[11]

But theories can be beguiling, and scientists are not immune to a bit of self-deception when a pet theory is at stake. Sometimes ideological considerations can be a strong bias, as we have seen in the case of eugenics. Often theories are premature, coming long before observations are available that may confirm or contradict them.

This was the case when Greek philosophers first began to theorize about nature. Beginning about 600 B.C. with Thales of Miletus, the so-called pre-Socratic philosophers asked questions that did not find answers until many centuries later. Their curiosity seemed unlimited, as was their faith in the power of the human intellect. Perhaps for the first time in human history the conviction was put forth that nature was not totally capricious, but that its course could be understood.

The questions asked went straight to the heart of everything that seemed puzzling: What is matter? How does it change? Or, more to the point, how is change possible? When a log burns and changes into smoke and ashes, does the log cease to exist? Are smoke and ashes created in its place?

Different schools gave different answers, but all saw in the element of change the mystery that is common to all physical phenomena. Without changes there would be nothing to explain. It was also a common theme that creation and destruction were fundamentally incomprehensible, and so these thinkers searched for something that could not change, that was preserved through all possible transformations.

Matter was always there. But was it possible that the smoke and the ashes were the same matter that made up the log? Thales thought so, and solved the puzzle of change with his theory that there was only one form of matter, one substance that could somehow take on different appearances. Later, the *pluralists* thought up a more plausible theory: There are several fundamental substances, each indestructible. The world of change merely reflected the mixing and rearranging of these elements in different proportions. Then there was the idea of atomicity: all matter consists of small invisible particles, each indivisible, hence the name atoms. No one atom could ever be created or destroyed. They moved through space that was otherwise empty. They occasionally collided with one another, became rearranged into different combinations and structures, and eventually separated again. But each atom was forever, and forever unchangeable.

Clearly the ancient theory of atoms provided the mind with an embarrassment of riches. Physical change no longer seemed mysterious. All observations seemed plausible now, and there was no further need to invoke supernatural agencies. The world became a machine. Past and future appeared linked together in a causal chain that was simple and inescapable, the interweaving of the trajectories of myriads of atoms.

In all these theories from Thales to the atomists, understanding is achieved through the recognition of some unchangeable quantity. This is still the approach in modern physics, where we speak of *conservation laws*. One of the oldest conservation laws, that of matter, has endured with little change ever since. This is why science has been called thinking about nature in the Greek — we should say the pre-Socratic — fashion.

The charming naïveté of the pre-Socratics, coupled with their unbridled intellectual zest, lasted barely two centuries. With Socrates the intellectual climate had taken a dramatic turn away from speculation about nature. Xenophon has this to report about Socrates:

> He did not even discuss that topic so favored by other talkers, "the Nature of the Universe," and avoided speculation on the so-called "Cosmos" of the Professors, how it works, and on the laws that govern the phenomena of the

heavens. Indeed, he would argue, that to trouble one's mind with such problems is sheer folly. In the first place, he would inquire, did these thinkers suppose that their knowledge of human affairs was so complete that they must seek these new fields for the exercise of their brains? . . . Students of human nature, he said, think that they will apply their knowledge in due course for the good of themselves and any others they choose. Do those who pry into heavenly phenomena imagine that, once they have discovered the laws by which these are produced, they will create at their will winds, waters, seasons and such things to their need? Or have they no such expectation, and are they satisfied with knowing the causes of these various phenomena? . . . His own conversation was ever of human things. The problems he discussed were What is godly, what is ungodly; what is beautiful, what is ugly; what is just, what is unjust; what is prudence, what is madness; what is courage, what is cowardice; what is a state, what is a statesman; what is government, and what is a governor. . . .[12]

The words of Socrates are prophetic in a way he did not intend. Scientists have indeed *not* been "satisfied with knowing the causes of these various phenomena," but have succeeded beyond all imagination to "create at their will winds, waters, seasons and such things to their need."

Today's civilization is so thoroughly technicized, so saturated with the means provided by science, that a return to a more primitive level is unthinkable and hardly desirable. Every significant advance in knowledge and know-how becomes woven into the fabric of our culture and cannot be taken out again without unraveling it all.

While we would like to remove some of the ugliest products of human invention — biological weapons, nerve gases, hydrogen bombs — we don't seem to be able to extricate ourselves from the power they have gained over us. We may destroy our arsenal of horrors, but we cannot destroy our ability to replenish them. Even ardent advocates of nuclear disarmament are aware that a world in which all nuclear weapons are destroyed is likely to be unstable because the fear of mutual assured destruction (MAD) has been the capstone in the delicate balance between the superpowers. The ready availability of nuclear weapons has thus served to suppress that potential spark of anger that could have set off a conflagration on a worldwide scale similar to that of the two world wars in the first — the prenuclear — half of this century.

It is a stopgap measure that cannot be expected to provide long-term security. The capstone is wired to detonate at any time. In the long run, nuclear destruction of mankind cannot be prevented by imminent threats, nor by the temporary abolition of nuclear weapons. If it came to a conflict, no power would be likely to contemplate military defeat rather than resorting to its most effective weapons, which it would not take long to reconstruct. Since we cannot destroy our know-how to replenish them, what must be destroyed is our willingness to inflict nuclear devastation on our adversaries *under any circumstances*.

In the meantime our arsenal of threats and counterthreats is becoming ever more destructive and ever more assured. It appears that in our pursuit of knowledge we have painted ourselves into a corner. N. O. Brown suggests madness as the only way out.

Of course there are still "pure scientists" who are unconcerned with practical uses of their labor, whose sole passion is to know and to understand the "mysteries of Nature," as Paracelsus put it. But there is no longer such a thing as "pure science," because every theory, every fact uncovered, sooner or later will find an application, and often that application may be the last thing the scientist contemplated.

The great cost of practically every scientific endeavor has made scientific research a political issue. Some of the studies we like to label *pure research* because they still seem removed from practical uses — astronomy, high energy physics — have become among the most expensive. The proposed *superconducting supercollider,* the SSC, is to accelerate elementary particles to energies not previously achieved in the laboratory, at a cost of some five billion dollars. It is designed to push exploration into the smallest realm of nature yet studied and promises to answer some questions that are at the very heart of contemporary science. The SSC will also provide a considerable economic lift to its chosen location and has therefore become the object of intense bidding and lobbying among a number of interested states.

Another multibillion dollar project is the proposed attempt to determine a detailed map of the human genome. It is called the "holy grail" of biology and is expected to take between ten and fifteen years, with an annual budget of around two hundred million dollars.

Guessing the future of science is risky business. Nobody could have anticipated that the discovery of the atomic nucleus at the beginning of the present century would in a few decades produce weapons that could threaten our very existence. But just as often we overestimate the progress of science. When atomic fission power became practical in the late forties, it seemed that power from nuclear fusion (controlled thermonuclear reactions) was just around the corner, and with it virtually limitless cheap energy, without the high risk inherent in nuclear fission plants and the enormous problem of disposal of radioactive wastes. Now, some forty years later, the best predictions are that we will not have fusion power until well into the twenty-first century.[13]

Some decades ago it seemed a safe guess that by the year 2000 infectious diseases would be a thing of the past. Immunizations and better sanitary conditions had all but eliminated the major causes of communicable death: smallpox, tuberculosis, polio. With antibiotics and high-tech birth control, sex had become almost worry-free. There was reason to be upbeat about medical science.

We were in for big shocks. In 1976 at an American Legion convention in Philadelphia, several persons died of Legionnaire's disease, an infection that had never before been observed. The culprit was a new bug that struck out from its shelter in the hotel's air-conditioning system. But the worst was still to come. A new virus, called HIV for *human immunodeficiency virus,* apparently hatched somewhere in Africa under still mysterious circumstances, made its appearance in the late seventies and spread worldwide within a few years.

Medical science was left in the embarrassing position of having to admit that it could not account for its arrival and had no means of curing the disease or preventing its spread. Its victims could only look forward to months of agony, followed by almost certain death. AIDS had terminated what one American writer called the only ten years of sexual freedom in all of human history.

Mind at the End of Its Tether?

That phrase was used by N. O. Brown, that advocate of Neoplatonism whose 1960 address at Columbia University we mentioned earlier. He borrowed the expression from H. G. Wells. By *mind* he meant rational mind. What he was saying was that the bridge science had built across the Cartesian cut had failed us, that the "fools with tools" — his expression for scientists — who are trying to lead mankind across, are false prophets, and that "only a miracle can save us." He calls for abandonment of rational mind, a rebirth of the spirit of Plato, and rekindling of a Dionysian frenzy, a "madness that comes from the God."[14]

Brown's solution may not appeal to us, but his question cannot be ignored. Is mind at the end of its tether?

There are reasons for arguing that it might be. To the man in the street the products of contemporary mind can be threatening. There is a sense of loss of control attending such innovations as H-bombs or genetic engineering. When not threatening, scientific discoveries often seem irrelevant or unreal or absurd.

Art, the other product of the human mind, does not always give us much comfort. Donoghue quotes the art critic Harold Rosenberg, who said "No one can say with assurance what a work of art is — or, more important, what is not a work of art. Where an art object is still present, as in painting, it is what I have called an anxious object: it does not know whether it is a masterpiece or junk."[15] A stroll through a gallery of contemporary art generally brings us face to face with a succession of such *anxious objects* to whose pleading gestures we are not able to give a reassuring nod. Art and artist also seem to strain at the end of their tether. The final verdict is not yet in whether the emperor has new clothes or is really naked. Trying to satisfy the constant demand for novelty of expression, art, many people feel, is decidedly straining at the end of a tether.

But science, too, has come up against new, unexpected limits, apart from its burgeoning cost and sometimes questionable utility. Once before, near the end of the nineteenth century, physicists thought that they had reached the end of their labors. Newtonian mechanics, together with the eminently successful theories of electrodynamics and statistical mechanics, formed a powerful and apparently all-encompassing body of knowledge. What remained to be studied seemed pedestrian by comparison, merely a matter of clearing up details. The excitement was over.

Then came the big surprises of the twentieth century: relativity, quantum mechanics, the esoteric and thoroughly non-Newtonian world of the very small, and the uncovering of a universe more mysterious and more grandiose than anything anyone dreamed of. Physics was once again a seemingly limitless playground for creative minds, with puzzles, obstacles, and contradictions wherever one looked.

Relativity solved some problems, quantum mechanics others, both at great cost to intuition. But no theory could consistently account for the whole range of observed phenomena. The giants of yesterday's modern physics — Einstein, Schroedinger, Heisenberg — all tried to fit together the various pieces of the puzzle, to arrive at a *unified theory* — and failed. At one point Max Born, another leading physicist of his time, predicted that "physics as we know it will be over in six months." That was in 1928.[16]

Today there is again a feeling in the air that completion may not be so far off. While acknowledging that many profound questions remain unanswered, some physicists are beginning to talk of a *theory of everything,* a grandiose unification that would contain all significant truths about nature. It may emerge when physicists find a common denominator for the four fundamental forces that are now recognized.[17] Perhaps the superconducting supercollider will help remove the last obstacles for such an understanding. And perhaps the hoped-for completeness is as illusory as was the last one.

The new attempts at grand unification are strange, mysterious structures. One of these, the theory of *superstrings,* has been criticized for offering virtually no predictions that can be verified by experiment, and yet would, in its completed form, answer all fundamental questions about the universe, account for all of its forces, all of its laws.

What are superstrings? To say that they are mathematical abstractions in ten dimensions does not help us much. They do have something to do with structure of matter and space at the smallest dimensions. We get an idea of the conceptual remoteness of superstrings when we consider their supposed size: if we were to enlarge everything to make superstrings the size of the nucleus of a single atom, the nucleus would become as big as the earth, and the earth the size of the entire universe.

Some physicists consider this a return to magic. Sheldon Glashow, a Harvard physicist and Nobel laureate for his work that successfully unified two of the four forces of nature, speaks derisively of superstring theories as "more appropriate to schools of divinity than to physics departments."[18]

But for Edward Witten of Princeton's Institute for Advanced Study, the physicist who is the theory's chief promoter, superstrings are "a piece of 21st century physics that fell by chance into the 20th century

. . . a few crumbs from the table compared to the feast which awaits us."[19]

In another sense, science is now confronted for the first time with a real barrier that seems to say: "This is the end. You cannot go beyond this point."

The physical universe, most physicists now agree, came into being between fifteen and twenty billion years ago. If present notions are correct, we can contemplate conditions that existed a minute fraction of a second following the *big bang*, the explosion that gave birth to the cosmic egg. There was a time when what appears now as the entire universe was the size of our earth, and before that the size of an orange, and before that the size of the head of a pin. That was about one thousandth of a billionth of a second after the beginning. Counting backwards through unimaginably small time intervals and conditions that can be described but not imagined, we can approach time zero, but we can never quite reach it. And we certainly cannot talk about anything *before* that cataclysmic event. Science comes to a halt there. The end of the tether. There is nothing on the other side that the human mind can grasp.[20]

But we don't have to go back in time. There is good reason to believe that similar limits to our understanding exist now. It appears more and more certain that at the center of our galaxy, and perhaps in most galaxies, there is an object that is utterly beyond our powers of description: a million or more suns collapsed into a single point — mathematicians call it a *singularity*, a *black hole*.

It has long been conjectured that, if gravitational forces exceeded a certain limit, matter would be crushed into nothingness. The mass would still be there, but it would occupy no space, and most of the laws we recognize in nature would be suspended. Here too, physics comes to an end.

Are science and magic once again moving toward a common ground? There are many advocates of such a view. Fritjof Capra, a University of California physicist, finds close parallels between modern physics and Eastern mysticism.[21] But others, like the brilliant Cambridge cosmologist and researcher on black holes Stephen W. Hawking, object to such "descent into wooliness."[22] To them science is incompatible with all forms of the supernatural (and that includes religions, mysticism, and such pseudoscientific endeavors as parapsychology).

Conscience and the Pursuit of Knowledge

Mind has its problems, but mindlessness is not the way out. Holy madness can have unholy consequences, and frenzy always has its victims. Unreason would be harmless except that it arms itself with the best that science and technology have to offer. Unlike their medieval counterparts, Urban II and Hakim the Mad (see p. 11), today's demagogues have their mindless phrases and faces bounced off orbiting satellites and instantly reassembled on picture tubes all over the globe. Science has been recruited to serve the meanest of tasks. It is not technology that is being questioned. It is *mind*.

For better or worse, we must accept the fact that the ability to reason has been the ecological niche of humans ever since our ancestors left the trees. It enabled early *Homo sapiens* to survive. It has committed us to a path of growing knowledge and skills, because they inevitably create new problems that necessitate further escalation in both knowledge and skills.

Some eighty years ago *Scientific American*, one of the oldest semipopular journals on science, had a news item on the then very new automobile. Lamenting the noisy clatter of horse-drawn wagons down city streets and the inevitable horse manure deposited daily on the pavements, it envisioned a bright future in which horseless carriages would glide by noiselessly on rubber wheels, leaving no pollution behind. The dream turned out differently. The roar of eighteen-wheelers down the freeways of modern cities makes us think nostalgically of the clatter of carriages, and the megapollution caused by millions of carbon-monoxide-belching automobile engines has become a major health problem.

Of course, we cannot go back and replace all engines by horses. The best we can do is to make quieter cars and try to reduce the noxious emissions. Technological civilization has no stable point in its progress, and the path is irreversible. We cannot retreat into blissful ignorance.

On the other hand, simple, unfettered curiosity, that has in the past been the mainspring of scientific advances, can no longer be sustained. The reasons are threefold: they are economical, practical, and ethical. It has simply become too expensive to follow our curiosity wherever it may take us. I have mentioned several multibillion dollar projects whose cost is now being weighed against potential benefits.

At the other extreme are practical problems that have to be pursued now out of sheer necessity: the escalating problems of industrial pollution, management of scarce resources, acute problems of public health, and many others. Finally, there are lines of research that raise fundamental ethical questions. Military research has come under severe scrutiny, especially the development of such means of mass destruction and indiscriminate killing as nuclear warheads, biological warfare, or nerve gas. Where do we draw the line between defensible means of defense and *offensive* offense?

Questions of ethics are not limited to military matters. They arise also in the field of medicine and public health. How much is it worth to save a human life? On whom shall we try new drugs and how soon? How much pain are we prepared to inflict on animals to further human health? How much pain on humans to delay their death?

We have stated the proposition that we cannot stop enlarging our knowledge and technological skills. But science has entered a new era, in which there is of necessity more control that is restrictive, coercive, and often seductive over what scientists are doing. The simple fact that practically all research needs funding by some agency, public or private, invests these agencies with enormous power. Government agencies, in particular, have almost total control over the type of research to be carried out and over who deserves to be the investigator. Only in the medical field is official wisdom supplemented by private fund drives. But these are restricted to the talked-about diseases like cancer, heart disease, or muscular dystrophy. (Nobody has attempted to stir up public sentiment and private financial support for research on syphilis or gonorrhea.) Nonmedical research is almost entirely dependent on governmental largess. Imagine a fund drive to investigate sunspots!

The power of governmental purse strings almost amounts to a realization of Plato's call for "complete state control" of science. The *state,* fortunately, is a very complex system with many checks and balances and even occasional wisdom mixed in with a lot of foolishness and ineptitude. Decision making has become a curious combination of individual and collective choices. To improve the wisdom of the decisions it would be desirable that the decision makers at all levels be the most intelligent, well-meaning, and the best informed. We are clearly a long way from this ideal.

The dilemma faced by science is not all imposed from above. It begins when the student of science chooses his or her field of interest and expertise. Here the self-image of the scientist, his natural interests and inclinations, face some harsh questions. Are talents matched to ambitions? Are the professional ambitions compatible with other necessities and desired life-style? And, most important, will there be opportunities to practice what he or she has spent years training for? Every year multitudes of graduating scientists are pushed by economic considerations into activities they don't find interesting and for which they are often poorly qualified. What is worse is that it often requires some effort on their part to convince themselves that what they are doing is of any benefit to society. The center of gravity of research is shifted toward "where the money is" (or the best climate, or the best sailing).

The direction of growth of knowledge, its conscious and conscientious control, is of vital concern to the survival of any technological society. It often seems that the choices are beyond the individual. In the *collectivist model,* society has developed a *supermind* that directs the flow of human affairs. The individual can only try to fit in. To the *individualist,* consciousness is never collective, and all important decisions are conscious decisions. They are made by individuals.

Perhaps the controversy between collectivists and individualists is academic. The acquisition of knowledge is both an individualistic and a collectivist enterprise. We need wise men and women in policy-making positions to make the vital decisions. But wise people are chosen, and must be supported, by a well-informed public. Today's best scientists, like all their predecessors, are highly individualistic. They are neither the good-natured stumblebums of so many TV caricatures nor half-deranged Dr. Strangeloves. What is new is their immeasurably greater potential for doing good or harm and the greater control society exerts over their activities. Their collective responsibility rests on their individual judgment and integrity, which in turn must operate within the confines of public policies.

But how is public policy to be determined? Appropriations for research are made by the budget committee of the U.S. Congress, which must decide whether to fund or not to fund such ventures as development of a space station (expected cost about $30 billion), expanded AIDS research ($20 billion), research into the feasibility of fusion reactors ($20 billion), as well as such minor "big science" projects as the previously mentioned superconducting supercollider and the mapping of the human genome (both in the multibillion dollar range).

Much will depend on those decisions. Failure to fund may prove disastrous in some cases, while decisions to fund may detract from other, worthier, causes and turn out to be money wasted. Senator Proxmire, before his retirement, had become notorious for his annual Golden Fleece Award to the most wasteful research project. It is generally felt among scientists that he was playing to the galleries. An uninformed public is easily persuaded that a project with a title like "The Mating Habits of the African Clawed Toad" means that their tax dollars are being frivolously poured down a sinkhole. It could be, however, that the research is concerned with questions whose significance transcends the silly-sounding title. Was the senator really qualified to make that decision?

One may think that the best alternative would be to fund all projects that perceivably have a direct and desirable bearing on society, so-called *applied research,* leaving the remainder of the budget — if there is any — for the investigation of fundamental scientific problems, that is, the mere satisfaction of scientific curiosity. There is always pressure in that direction from the more pragmatically minded. History has shown that this would be a short-sighted policy, since many of the more revolutionary technological advances of the past have come out of such *basic research.*

This has put legislators in a quandary, the more so since in the past, scientific organizations, such as the National Academy of Sciences, have refused to become engaged in advocating scientific priorities. Congress has recently been asking for more advice from the scientific community, and Dr. Robert M. Rosenzweig, president of the Association of American Universities, has warned against "uninformed and dangerous decisions by our government."[23]

It used to be said that science is a search for truth, and that truth is both objective and ethically neutral. But scientists are not objective, and they would be a menace if they were ethically neutral. The critical dependence of our society on the activities of scientists demands closer interaction between the two and a new cultivation of trust. Scientists, of course, are no more infallible than senators, and their opinions are as diverse. All prognostication is risky, but if we engage the best-informed members of our society, it will be a lot better than proceeding blindly, or following the suggestions of special-interest groups, or — as has been the policy under a recent administration — by horoscope.

Errors in judgment have become expensive. We must learn to step gingerly, because knowledge can also become a minefield. Some truths are urgently needed, others should never have been uncovered. Mankind has no need to know how to improve the adhesive quality of napalm to the human skin or the most efficient way to defoliate a forest.

Heinz von Foerster, a professor emeritus at the University of Illinois, Urbana, expressed it well: "Invoking objectivity is abrogating responsibility, whence comes its popularity."[24] And the explosive growth of knowledge lays on all of us an almost unbearable responsibility.

CHAPTER VIII

Language: The Artful Weapon

IT HAS BEEN OVER FORTY YEARS since George Orwell wrote *1984*, that shocking prophecy of the ultimate oppression of the individual by the state. Mankind approached the year 1984 with some trepidation. But it turned out to be no worse than its predecessors. There were pockets of armed conflict scattered over the globe, the usual areas of intense religious and ethnic hostilities, terrorism and counterterrorism, a patchwork of areas of plenty and of famine, saber rattling by the superpowers, and a dawning realization that the facilities of the planet Earth, both as a source of sustenance and as a dumping ground for our waste, were finite after all.

Fortunately, Orwell's worst predictions had not come to pass. The word *freedom* still retained its meaning, even where it was in short supply. Orwell's novel nevertheless taught us an important lesson. The chief instrument of oppression in *1984* was language. The state, under Big Brother, had replaced the English tongue with a mindless babble, called Newspeak, whose purpose it was to deprive thought of any linguistic foothold in unwanted territory. Undesirable thoughts were purged by deleting the words, or at least the meanings that could express them:

The word *free* still exists in Newspeak, but it could only be
used in such statements as "This dog is free of lice" or "This
field is free of weeds." It could not be used in its old sense of
"politically free" or "intellectually free," since political and
intellectual freedom no longer existed even as concepts, and
were therefore of necessity nameless.[1]

It was appropriate for Orwell to single out language as the means to
achieve total control over mind and body. In our survey of man's arsenal of wits, nothing stands out as prominently as his ability to turn
mind into communication. And nothing is as effective in enslaving the
mind as the clever abuse of language.

Paradoxically, language begins as soliloquy. A child's first sen-
tences, we are told, are addressed to himself. Talking to oneself is an
activity practiced by humans of all ages. There is something preposter-
ous about the idea of telling oneself something one evidently knows
already. But the activity is not as absurd as all that. What apparently
happens is that an idea is conceived in the brain. At first nebulous and
inexpressible, it swirls through the jungle of neurons, where it is
sampled, savored, elaborated, and sometimes made audible. The word
is caught again by the nervous system and deciphered, and new meaning is attached. The earliest function of language is thus to serve as an
anchor point in that self-referent creative loop that is the mind.

This bootstrap character of language was realized over a century
ago. By then it had become apparent that the language ability of humans depended on two structures in the left hemisphere of the cerebral cortex, Broca's area in the frontal lobe and Wernicke's area in the
temporal lobe of the brain. The first is generally associated with the
generation of speech, the second with its comprehension, although
today's neuroscientists no longer believe in the strict localization of
these functions. A lesion in Broca's area causes difficulty in forming
words (*motor aphasia*), and damage in Wernicke's area leads to *sensory aphasia:* the patient hears the words but fails to comprehend
their meaning. It was found that most patients in the latter group also
have speech impairment. William James, in his seminal work *The
Principles of Psychology,* first published in 1890, explains this by saying that ". . . our ideas do not innervate our motor centers directly, but
only after arousing the mental sound of the words."[2] We sample our
thoughts by listening to ourselves — soliloquy innervating the creative
loop.

We don't know when and how language began among our distant ancestors. The Neanderthals, although often classified as *Homo sapiens,* were probably not capable of speech as we know it. Fossil evidence suggests that they did not possess the anatomical prerequisites to produce the rich variety of sounds required to keep pace with the brain's ruminations. This may have been their undoing. For their contemporaries, the Cro-Magnons, showed by their skull configurations that they had the equipment for talking.

Views differ concerning the first appearance of that unique ability about one hundred and fifty thousand years ago. According to one, represented by Noam Chomsky and his school of linguistics, the organs of speech and the brain centers controlling them have no precursors. They appear suddenly and in their present form. Language descended upon the hominids like a gift from heaven, a *creation,* rather than a product of evolution.

But most scientists shy away from Creationism of any kind. Philip Lieberman, a professor of cognitive and linguistic sciences at Brown University, sees language as the end product of a long history of evolutionary processes.[3] Crucial changes had to take place in the anatomy of the larynx, the oral and nasal passages, and the delicate musculature controlling it all. The organ of the control, Broca's area, in the frontal cortex, presumably evolved along with these changes. The severity of the requirement is gleaned from this example given by Lieberman: Think of the rhythmic tapping of a pencil on a tabletop. At low frequencies we can distinguish every tap, but at fifteen taps a second and beyond, we perceive only a continuous buzz. But our cortical speech area has no difficulty in selecting discrete speech commands at the rate of twenty-five a second, the muscles lining our respiratory system have no difficulty shaping the corresponding phonemes at the same rate, and the sensory apparatus located in Wernicke's area can distinguish every phoneme in that buzz and link them all into a meaningful whole.

It seems unlikely that this remarkable biological achievement occurred all at once. It is a good guess that toolmaking could not have become a widespread practice without the art of communication through speech. But some rudimentary language may have existed long before the first flint was struck, and perhaps the first words, like those of today's children, were spoken in isolation.

It may be that language began as every individual's private tongue, intelligible to no other human, a Babel of voices without communication.

Siblings often share a private language. Gradually, through imitation, the first scattered islands of understanding may have emerged. Imitation and translation then must have created widening circles of communication.

"To learn to speak is to learn to translate," said Octavio Paz, the Mexican poet and essayist.[4] The translatability of human speech is a remarkably unifying fact. Paz tells us how, around the first century A.D., the Chinese, having discovered Buddhism in Peshawar and Kashmir, had gone through enormous hardships to transport the Sanskrit texts to China and render them in Chinese. "The school of translators was a school of travelers and explorers."

The translation Paz refers to is not just changing one tongue into another. Communication through language involves translating meaning into words and words back into meaning. The human minds at the two ends of that chain have the capacity of being uniquely and universally attuned to each other's signals, but the process is delicate and can easily be perverted. Some of the most tragic conflicts in human history can be traced to a breakdown of the process through error or by design.

If soliloquy is indeed the first stage of language, it continues to be an essential ingredient in our thought processes. In a sense, language is always part soliloquy. When we talk, we hear ourselves talking, and we talk to please ourselves.

But soliloquy has its pitfalls. The very nature of being self-referent, *recursive,* means that we can easily be led astray by our own language. Prejudice and anger become magnified and our own motives sanitized. We convince ourselves that we are doing the right thing and that our adversaries act from the basest of instincts. We can be gullible creatures and talk ourselves into almost anything. Our natural guard of skepticism drops away when we are both speaker and listener, and the resulting positive feedback can give rise to a runaway delusion.

Stuart Chase, in his *Tyranny of Words,* remarked that "poor humanity is not indulging so much in moral failure as in bad language."[5] What is bad in language, according to Chase, quite apart from inadequate usage, is its very structure.

Does language serve us well? We often grope for words. We often sputter. Sometimes we do both at once. Is language too rich or too poor? Are there too many words whose meanings are ambiguous, obscure, or nonexistent? We take for granted that every word has a referent, and that every string of words describes relations between real referents. Would perhaps the elimination of such words as *soul* relieve us of much unwarranted philosophizing and *soulsearching*? Should we then prune our language down to a more Spartan vocabulary? Or are there too few words to express the full range of our sensations and emotions? Are the words at our disposal the inventors of feelings we would not otherwise have? Would we, as Orwell suggested in *1984*, lose our desire for freedom if the word *freedom* were expurgated and forgotten?

I quoted from the oration of Pope Urban II by which he incited the mindless fury of the Crusades (p. 12). In 1802, Ezra Sampson, referring to the English politician John Wilkes, published a treatise with the provocative title, *The Sham Patriot Unmasked, or An Exposition of the Fatally Successful Arts of Demagogues.* "Human nature," Sampson states:

> is the same sort of fluff now, that it was two or five thousand
> years ago. . . . By ardent appeals to passion and to avarice,
> those strings of the human heart are struck, which never fail
> to reverberate to the slightest touch. Though this trick, by its
> frequency, had become stale, long before the flood, it still
> succeeds, with only a little variation in its varnish and management.[6]

The Semantics Experiment

More than half a century ago, a movement to purge language of ambiguity and to lay bare the true meanings of words was begun in the United States by Count Alfred Korzybski. It was called *general semantics*. In 1933, Korzybski, a scientist and philosopher of Polish birth, published an ambitious though somewhat murky work entitled *Science and Sanity*. A few years later, Stuart Chase's *The Tyranny of Words* followed closely in Korzybski's footsteps, but avoided the Count's obscurantism. In the introduction, Chase asks rhetorically:

> Does B know what A is talking about? Does A himself
> know clearly what he is talking about? How often do minds
> meet; how often do they completely miss each other? How
> many of the world's misfortunes are due to such misses?[7]

The general semanticists saw the remedy in the language of science, specifically that of physics and mathematics. Physics was then riding on a wave of spectacular successes. The new discipline of quantum mechanics placed totally new demands on language, since intuition had to be largely abandoned. *Logical positivism,* a philosophy that was first conceived in Vienna by a group known as the Vienna Circle, seemed particularly attractive, since it did away with some of the more troubling questions by declaring them invalid. Only direct observation counts as reality, and theory is merely a way of organizing reality. Nothing is surmised. There is a joke about two logical positivists who pass a pasture where black sheep are grazing. "Look," says one, "all these sheep are black." "On one side, anyway," corrects the other.

In the United States, logical positivism was popularized by the physicist-philosopher Percy W. Bridgman, who coined the term *operational approach:* a quantity or object is defined by the *operations* we have to perform to ascertain it. Thus, to define the mass of an object you simply listed the operational steps required to determine it, just as the operational definition of French onion soup is simply the recipe for making it. There is no other, deeper, meaning to *mass.* Since we could not define *soul* operationally, the word is meaningless. We might as well strike it from our vocabulary.

Korzybski and Chase go beyond that. The *structure* of a language, they say, must correspond to the physical structure that it describes. Most languages, Chase states, are "structurally dissimilar to our nervous system and our environment." The result is confusion. Chase suggests a way out:

> There is, however one language which is capable of expressing the structural relations found in the known world and in the nervous system. . . . The name of this useful, well-ordered language is mathematics.[8]

It is not clear what Chase meant by "structural similarities" between our environment, the nervous system, and mathematics. General semantics, for all its praise of mathematical precision, is often a turgid doctrine. Its founder, Count Korzybski, ended up a cult figure in the early forties and was all but forgotten by the fifties. Little more than the term *semantics* survives to make us a little more aware of the hidden (or absent) meaning of some words. The ambitious attempt to create a language that speaks to us with the unambiguous clarity of a mathematical equation has proved to be a failure, however.

Fifty years after what was to be the semantic revolution, we are more than ever mired in clichés and as buffeted by empty oratory. The word has not become clearer, only louder. Far from having acquired anything like a mathematical precision, language is still everyone's fling at being an artist. And like all arts, language has its masters, its hacks, and its charlatans.

Language has, if anything, become more *anti*-semantic: the objective is frequently to steer the reader or listener away from the true content of the message — if there is one. During the Vietnam War, an air attaché at the U.S. embassy in Pnompenh complained to reporters: "You always write it's bombing, bombing, bombing. It's not bombing. It's *air support.*" The Chrysler Corporation described the layoff of 5,000 workers at its Wisconsin plant as a *career alternative enhancement program,* and General Motors referred to the closing of its Framingham, Massachusetts plant as a *volume related schedule adjustment.* "We had to reduce the size, because we didn't want to increase the price," boasted a candy manufacturer by way of explaining the paltry size of its chocolate bar.

Apart from such deliberate attempts at obfuscation, there is, however, a deeper reason why the semantics experiment had to fail. Language is not just a passive medium into which information is encoded, but an entity with its own dynamics that shape and transform both speaker and listener. Almost never a matter of pure logic, language provides a canvas, a medium for a multitude of arts and crafts that range from filibusters to Zen koans. If precision were the criterion of excellence, then insurance policies and computer manuals would represent the best in language. The fact is that most of us are bowled over by the simplest exercises in logic and baffled by syllogisms. String a few negatives together and we are lost. When it comes to communication, we are all artists, each with a characteristic approach, style, motivation, and choice of coloring. Words are not like coins whose values are fixed. Beside their multiple lexical meanings, they function in metaphors that are limited only by the inventiveness of the user. Thus, meanings are almost always extrinsic, depending, in ways that cannot be defined, not just on the words around them, but on the changing *world* around them. We learned that lesson when we first tried to "teach" a computer to translate from one language into another. "Pure logic," remarked the famous French mathematician Henri Poincaré, "could never lead to anything but tautologies."

Denis Donoghue had this to say about language: "What is common to poet and ordinary man is gibberish, a limping or spluttering translation of a feeling or an intuition we have to think of as aboriginal or otherwise beneath or above our syntax."[9]

The experiment of general semantics was a failure, and we still don't fully understand why it was a failure. One thing is clear, however: the knowledge required to translate a text, or just to render it intelligible, is vastly greater than what is contained in any dictionary. Meanwhile we continue to limp and splutter, and some of us question our ability ever to understand one another.

The New Barbarians

The word *barbarian* is believed to have been coined by ancient Greeks to refer to anyone who spoke a strange, unintelligible tongue that to them sounded like so much *bah bah*. Barbarians appeared to be babblers.

But foreign tongues can be made intelligible through the art of translation, whereas true babblers either convey nothing or use their language to obfuscate, incite, or seduce. Babble comes in many genres: there is psychobabble, diplobabble, technobabble, adbabble, and many others. The National Council of Teachers of English has had since 1970 a Committee on Public Doublespeak, which, among other activities, selects a recipient for the annual Doublespeak Award. In 1987 that honor went to Lieutenant Colonel Oliver North and Admiral John Poindexter for contributing to the worsening pollution of our language and for their outstanding ability to clothe unpleasant truths in attractive garb.

The last decade, in particular, has spawned a whole new vocabulary of political obfuscation. There is the art of *maintaining plausible deniability,* which in oldspeak might have been called "covering your tracks and lying through your teeth." *Disinformation* is the deliberate spreading of lies through official channels, and *spin control* means throwing mud in the eyes of the observer to make him doubt the calamity he sees before him. It is now liberally used by government and industry. When the Long Island Lighting Company (Lilco) conducted a safety drill on its Shoreham Nuclear Plant, fifty-seven of the eighty-nine sirens that were to warn the population of a major nuclear accident and initiate evacuation of the area failed to function. A Lilco spokesman explained it this way:

> It's important to realize that having the sirens sound on the day of the exercise wasn't in the prescribed scenario. It was just an extra thing we put in. We had tested the sirens a week ago, and they were all working fine, and we tested them again, actually, this morning, and eighty-six of the eighty-nine sirens worked properly. So it was extremely unlikely that they wouldn't work then, although they didn't, and we are looking into why that equipment failed. But that's all really moot, because the *sirens* weren't being tested. *We* were being tested. At a later date, if we have a test that includes the sirens, and they don't go off, why, then we'll get a failing grade.[10]

That is spin control. William Safire, a keen observer and analyst of the spreading abuse of language, coined the expression "postvarication." Unlike *prevarication,* to which the term alludes, postvarication is

> the technique of setting forth an untruth in such a way that the listener will later find that the postvaricator had not actually been lying. Indeed, this verbal device, frequently used in Washington and other political capitals, includes a deliberate signal to the listener that less than the truth is being told.[11]

The question whether a particular official knew about some misdeed committed by his office is often answered with the phrase that he "hadn't been fully informed," which is compatible with "I knew very well what was going on, except for some insignificant detail that may have escaped me." That, of course, is not what the postvaricator is trying to convey. Safire points out that the statement "We have no such plan at this time" may well mean "Get ready."

Some of the above examples may be amusing, but the progressive deterioration of language poses a threat to humanity as real as the atom bomb, or the population bomb, or global pollution.

The Language Bomb

World War II and the Holocaust were the direct consequences of Hitler's consummate skills as a demagogue. The devastating potential of the word is all around us, mostly unrecognized. This is especially true in the language of international politics, where it usually aggravates the differences between *us* and *them*.

It is customary to have two separate dictionaries, each containing the synonyms of the other, but having very different emotional impact. In dictionary one, which we use to describe *their* actions, we find words like "terrorist" or "naked aggression." Dictionary two shows "freedom fighter" and "preemptive defensive action" in corresponding places. These expressions are used when we talk about what *we* do.

The most disturbing aspect of this perversion of language is its effect on international law and treaties. The words they contain were designed as a bulwark against chaos and lawlessness. If we tamper with their meaning, we destroy the protection that wiser men sought to provide for us.

The Biological Weapons Convention, signed by the United States and the USSR in 1972, is a case in point. The agreement made it illegal to carry out further development of new biological weapons. It was prompted in part by the revulsion against subjecting civilian populations to airborne plagues or wholesale death by nerve gas. Nevertheless, under the Reagan administration, funding for the so-called biological defense program has increased from $16 million to $75 million per year. Part of this paid for research and *production* of new types of biological weapons. It was held that this was not a violation of the treaty, since the avowed purpose of these weapons was merely to enable us to design appropriate countermeasures. "You can't test bullet-proof vests," someone said, "unless you first make bullets."

The ABM Treaty makes another case study of the crumbling of a treaty when its language is turned into *doublespeak*. The Antiballistic

Missile Treaty, signed by the United States and the USSR in 1972, imposes strict limits on testing of space weapons. The purpose was to forestall the development by either side of an effective shield against nuclear warheads. It was felt that such a development would upset an already precarious balance by encouraging further escalation in the number of nuclear weapons, or even enable one side to launch a first strike.

The treaty became an obstacle to the Strategic Defense Initiative (SDI), started in the Reagan era and popularly known as "star wars." In 1985, Abraham D. Sofaer, a lawyer for the State Department, at the urging of the Pentagon revealed the so-called broad interpretation of the ABM Treaty, which would allow unlimited testing of space weapons based on "new physical principles." It is significant that, with one exception, all original negotiators of the treaty disagree with Sofaer's interpretation of their language. The obvious meaning of the language of the treaty — and the meaning evidently intended by most of the negotiators — now became the traditional, or narrow, interpretation. Under the traditional interpretation testing of space weapons is curtailed; under the broad interpretation it is not.

In a bizarre extension of this battle of interpretations, doublespeak was turned into quadruplespeak. Ashton B. Carter, a former Harvard professor, has pointed out that the traditional interpretation is really not as restrictive as people think it is, but would actually allow the kind of testing for which they thought the broad interpretation was needed. We may call this bit of sophistry the broad interpretation of the traditional interpretation. There is also a narrow interpretation of the broad interpretation, which goes as follows: testing of space-based interceptors would indeed be allowed if they employed other, that is, new physical principles. But the technology of the proposed SDI systems existed when the ABM Treaty was signed. Hence no testing under the broad interpretation![12]

I mention the examples of the Biological Weapons Convention and the ABM Treaty because of the particularly critical role of language in international affairs. Unfortunately, it is there, especially, that doublespeak has become *rubberspeak,* where language can be stretched to have almost any meaning. We have blurred the distinction between such opposites as war and peace, aggression and defense, right and wrong. We can, against all accepted principles of international law, finance and orchestrate insurrections against legitimate foreign governments, including arranging for heads of state to be assassinated.

When preceded by appropriate oratory, this process, called *destabilization,* is generally applauded, and only the most perfunctory deniability need be maintained.

The wonder is how readily we can be swayed by words. Demagoguery is rarely forced on us. We seek and worship our Pied Pipers, who rubberbabble themselves into our hearts. They give us pleasure because they justify and nourish our fears, buttress our most outrageous beliefs, and flatter our sense of righteousness.

General semantics tried in vain to take art and mystery out of language and leave only hard logic. Our modern barbarians have deprived language of reason and turned it into junk art. It can sell cereals as readily as it promotes foreign adventures. "We reduced the size because we didn't want to increase the price" goes down as smoothly as that famous announcement following the saturation bombing of a Vietnamese village: "We had to destroy the village in order to save it."

CHAPTER IX

Life Span of a Technological Civilization

IN THE INTRODUCTION I touched on the question of survival in a changing world. Like the tube worms and giant clams near the hydrothermal vents at the bottom of the Pacific Ocean, we are dependent, at least temporarily, on the bounty of a circumscribed local environment, our planet Earth. Surrounding us is the emptiness of space and, within a few hundred million miles, a handful of planets, all uninhabitable unless thoroughly modified. Apart from a few brief forays into this hostile world, mankind has been bound to this Earth, for better or worse.

Visionaries often point to space as the solution to many of our problems. We are told that we will have solved the problem of overpopulation once we have succeeded in colonizing space. The resources of our own solar system are virtually unlimited: energy, warmth, scarce materials to supply our industries are there for the asking. And the vastness of space can hold all the detritus of our civilization from garbage to radioactive waste for eons to come.

Why, then, the concern about our future? The answer is that our problems are more imminent than the solutions that outer space may provide.[1]

The human population has reached the five billion mark some time during 1987 and will pass six billion before the year 2000. To keep the Earth's population at its present already crowded level we would have to ship into outer space a billion people — something like the entire population of China — in a little over a decade, or eighty-five million people a year! With the present doubling time of forty years, the total number of people alive would soar to fifty billion by the year 2200. At that time, with the policy of exporting the surplus, and allowing for equal fecundity in space, every planet in our solar system would have reached our present level of five billion people. If we could solve the transportation problem, it is doubtful that we could construct enough habitable and self-sufficient space to accommodate such numbers in so short a time. Of course, a more realistic outlook would envision no significant space colonization within the next century, instead only the tragic overcrowding of Earth.

Some scientists have even derived a *doomsday equation,* which closely matches population statistics over more than a thousand years of the past and predicts that sometime around the year 2026 the number of people would equal infinity.[2] Since this is a physical impossibility, it would simply mean the end of humanity. Such forecasts have occasioned an epitaph exhibited at the Bishop Museum in Honolulu, Hawaii, that reads:

IN MEMORY OF

MAN

2,000,000 BC–AD 2030

HE ONCE DOMINATED

THE EARTH

DESTROYED IT

WITH HIS WASTES

HIS POISONS AND

HIS OWN NUMBERS

The doomsday equation is to be taken seriously but not quite so literally. The explosive growth of the population is bound to be broken within the next few decades, by mass starvation, disease, or by nuclear warfare, unless we take some drastic and more humane steps to limit our numbers in the very near future.

The other promissory benefits of space travel, the mining of scarce materials on the moon or on the asteroids, and the disposal of waste, may come to pass sometime in the future but are no help in our short-range outlook. The transportation problem is staggering and would be far too costly to solve. Consider that New York State alone generates 48,000 tons of trash in just one day, not counting the prodigious amounts of treated sewage that are dumped almost daily into the Atlantic just off the continental shelf.

Drake's Seventh Term

Most scientists scoff at stories about flying saucers, and with good reason. Reports of sightings are ill-documented and anecdotal, which means they are based on single, nonreproducible events that leave no permanent, generally verifiable evidence. But most of all, the whole thing makes no sense. Why should all these extraterrestrial gumshoes hover around Earth in their spaceships decade after decade without having made one confirmed contact or leaving one shred of hard evidence?

The possible existence of extraterrestrial intelligence, however, is quite another matter. Most scientists would readily concede this possibility, and many are now involved in a serious attempt to scan the cosmic radio noise for messages sent by intelligent beings from the vicinity of some distant star. The SETI project (Search for Extra-Terrestrial Intelligence) is a serious scientific undertaking that has been quietly pursued for a number of years.

The reason for this apparent paradox is that, unlike the reported visitations by flying saucers, the existence of intelligence elsewhere in the universe makes excellent sense. This has to do with the growing conviction that a large fraction of stars in our galaxy may have planetary systems not unlike our own sun's. Among all these planets there will be some that are comparable to our Earth in chemical composition and climatic conditions. Further, if the origin of life is an event that has a high likelihood of occurring when conditions are favorable, we may anticipate that many of these planets sustain life. Finally, given a benevolent environment and enough time, we believe that chances are high for evolution to lead to beings capable of developing a culture and, eventually, a technology. At a certain level of civilization, they may wonder, as we do, whether other intelligent life is "out there," and decide to beam encoded messages into space. Our large radiotele-scopes are today scanning likely regions in space in the hope of pick-ing up such a message. When they do we would know that we are not alone in the universe.

Such messages, duly recorded by scientific teams, perhaps in more than one place, could then be analyzed exhaustively for authenticity and content. Also, it is unlikely that there would be only a single brief message. Instead, once the location of the suspected source in the sky is established, dozens of radio-observatories could turn their instru-ments to that spot in the heavens to confirm what would be the great-est discovery of all ages.

A few dedicated scientists have been involved in the SETI project, so far without success. But the effort has been sporadic, and the chances of tuning in at the right frequency — there are millions of possible channels — and looking in the right location in the sky are slim. The goal is sufficiently tempting, however, for NASA to plan a concerted and well-funded effort that is to last for ten years, starting on Columbus day 1992, five hundred years after the discovery of America.

Of course, no one knows how many other civilizations there are in our galaxy, if indeed there are any, besides our own, and whether they are sufficiently advanced to know about the technology of sending electromagnetic signals into space. An estimate of sorts can be ob-tained by what is known as Drake's equation.

Frank Drake, an American astronomer, expresses the number of such advanced civilizations as the product of seven terms, among which are such numbers as the probability that a planet has conditions favorable to life and the probability that life actually evolves, given these conditions. The last term, the seventh term in Drake's equation, is the most critical and also the least known: it is the average life expectancy of a technological civilization. If that time span is long — perhaps millions or billions of years — then the likelihood is high that there are many advanced civilizations existing now. If, on the other hand, that time is short, such civilizations may have existed in the past but have long since perished. Each such civilization would have been like a brief flash in the long history of the universe, isolated in space and in time.

To estimate Drake's seventh term, we have only our own example to guide us. We have been at that communicable stage of technological advance for less than a century, and our future is precarious. How can we predict whether our life expectancy is another hundred years, or a thousand, a million, or perhaps a billion years? I will content myself here with a look at the more immediate future.

"The end of the twentieth century," says sociobiologist C. J. Lumsden, "will be the Great Age of the Mind." It is to be devoutly hoped that he is right, for mind will be our most precious commodity. So far, our minds are still tradition bound and barely aware of where we are heading. There are many ways our civilization could come to grief in the next few decades. Let us review some of these.

The Thermonuclear Finale

The most talked about ending is all-out nuclear war. This scenario is not idle speculation. The missiles are sitting in their silos, their engines ready, their navigation programmed. Nuclear-powered submarines are patrolling along well-defined sea lanes, their missiles waiting only for the command to be launched, and fleets of supersonic bombers are standing by to complete the destruction. Every major American and Soviet city is targeted.

All the difficult tasks have been accomplished: thermonuclear devices of all sizes and purposes have been designed, built, tested. The delivery systems have been perfected. All the tedious research and development, the funds to be appropriated, the contracts to be written, the building, the testing and final installation, and the state-of-the-art network of communication to keep it all in readiness. All that work is behind us. Like the final ceremonial ribbon-cutting on a completed construction project, it would take only a few keys to be turned, a few buttons pushed, to have it all go gloriously into operation.

That, of course, is not the avowed purpose of all this effort. Nuclear weapons advocates tell us that it is the mutual assured destruction which has given us four decades — not exactly of peace — but four decades without a major collision between the hostile superpowers. This success, the same people tell us, gives us confidence that a balance of terror is one of the two ways of insuring continued stability. The other, preferable to the first, is heavy imbalance in our favor.

Since we are benevolent, it would be desirable to achieve intimidating superiority of such magnitude that no adversary would dare act against our interests, let alone attack us.

The activities of both camps in this game have been directed during these four decades toward achieving the second solution, while maintaining the first as a minimal temporary goal.

It would be foolish to deny the deterrent value of nuclear weapons. But they have not produced stability. The arms race resulting from our striving for the second solution has led to enormous sacrifices of resources on both sides, while placing our security in the hands of a burgeoning technology over which we are rapidly losing control.

This new, dangerous instability is illustrated on a small scale by the two instances in which civilian airliners have become victims to a technology that has overwhelmed its keepers.

In 1983 Soviet planes downed Korean Airlines Flight 007, with the loss of 269 innocent lives. The action was labeled "pure barbarism" by our government. The possibility of an honest error on the part of the Russian pilot was not even contemplated. The Russians, in turn, accused us of using a civilian aircraft to spy on their territory, not conceding an honest navigational error by the Korean pilot.

Five years later, on July 2, 1988, the American guided-missile cruiser *Vincennes*, on duty in the Persian Gulf, fired a missile at Iranian Airlines Flight 655. Two hundred ninety civilian lives were lost. The Aegis weapons system of the *Vincennes*, considered to be the most sophisticated combination of radar, electronics, and guided missiles, mistook the regularly scheduled airbus flying within its assigned corridor for an F14 fighter plane. Our Defense Department labeled the downing of the airbus a "justifiable defensive posture."

If we are to believe the official pronouncements of our investigating teams, the Iranian Airlines Flight 655 was blown out of the sky not because of any malfunction of Aegis, which is designed to control airspace around its carrier over a range of more than 200 miles. The information was all there, properly coded, and displayed in the darkened control room of the *Vincennes* on large, glowing multicolored screens. A team of twenty-five highly trained officers and technicians were standing by.

We can only guess at the psychological drama that unfolded in the control room as the Iranian airbus, flying at 12,000 feet, climbing, and well within its assigned air corridor, rapidly closed the few remaining miles between it and our missile cruiser. There, it was not an airbus carrying 290 lives, but a menacing radar blip on the Aegis screens. The memory of another American naval vessel that, just a few months earlier, had taken a direct hit from an Iraqi plane and suffered heavy casualties must have weighed on the minds of commander and crew of the *Vincennes*.

Meanwhile, the electronic oracle of the Aegis system was spewing out its cryptic messages at an alarming rate, and the blip, a mere twelve miles distant, was closing in at the rate of ten miles in every sixty seconds.

Human brains are not wired for such speeds and such informational deluge. As the fateful seconds ticked away, somebody made the decision that the oracle had identified the blip as an attacking Iranian jet. One can almost sense the relief, the eager acceptance of the judgment that allowed them to end that intolerable tension with a few words spoken into the intercom, and the push of a few buttons . . .

The example of the drama on the *Vincennes* raises an important question: is it possible that our technology has become too sophisticated for our poor ancient brains? The possibility cannot be dismissed lightly. Technology is cumulative, growing through the addition of many small contributions, while intelligence, the source of this steady growth, remains fixed. At a certain point, we may find ourselves overwhelmed by our creations, when the intelligence required to achieve a certain level of technology may be less than that needed to survive it.

We have had other examples of such a mind–machine mismatch. The shooting down of the Korean Airlines Flight 007 in 1983 by Soviet fighter planes, the nuclear "accidents" at Chernobyl and Three Mile Island, are all examples in which humans had to interact with sophisticated machines. In all these cases it was the humans who failed.

Meanwhile we are entrusting the delicate balance of the nuclear standoff to just such an uncertain alliance. How many times in the past have nervous radar operators in their subarctic listening posts mistaken a flight of geese for incoming missiles? We don't know, and officials are not likely to tell us. If we have been lucky in the past, how many more years can we expect this precarious condition to continue?

The situation is, of course, far from static. Technological advances continue in both offensive and defensive devices, most of them having destabilizing effects. As an example, the installation of Trident II missiles combines the short flight time of submarine-launched missiles with the accuracy of the best land-based ICBMs. This means that

Soviet hardened missile silos could be neutralized in a matter of five or six minutes. This may seem like progress to some but may prove to be a disastrous move in the cold-war game. The Russian reaction is best assessed by asking what we would do under similar circumstances. With the threat of losing all of our deterrent capabilities in a few minutes, there would be little time to double-check, to confirm reports of incoming missiles. We would, and in all probability *they* would resort to a scenario so frightening it has hardly been mentioned. It is called *launch-on-warning*.

If the present standoff seems hazardous, a launch-on-warning policy, once adopted by the superpowers, would drastically reduce the life expectancy of our civilization, not through any hostile intent, but because of the inherent weakness of the mind–machine link.

The Reagan administration's answer to the nuclear threat was an ambitious undertaking, begun in the early eighties, known as Strategic Defense Initiative (SDI), or star wars. We have already discussed (p. 131) its effect on our commitment to the 1972 ABM Treaty. The star wars project was launched with the promise that it would provide an effective shield protecting the American population in an all-out nuclear attack. It now appears that the decision was made following the assertion by one scientist, Dr. Edward Teller, that a single nuclear-powered X-ray laser weapon, called Super Excalibur, could "potentially shoot down the entire Soviet land-based missile force." He estimated that this wonder weapon might become operational in about three years.

This was challenged later by Roy D. Woodruff, the associate director for defense systems at Lawrence Livermore National Laboratory. Woodruff was then heading the nuclear design program that included work on Excalibur. He pointed out that Teller's overoptimistic assessment lacked any experimental foundation and led to a "systematic deception of the nation's top leadership." Soon thereafter Woodruff resigned from his position at Livermore.

Without prospect for an effective nuclear shield, our best hope now lies in disengagement from the hair-trigger situation we have been drawn into. Partial disarmament is certainly a step in the right direction, and we must applaud all efforts, such as the recent treaty to ban intermediate-range nuclear missiles. It is important to understand that the treaty provides only for the destruction of the missiles, not their nuclear cargo, and that no present plans envision a pullback from the position of mutual assured destruction, not even the 50 percent reduction in long-range nuclear ballistic missiles, which is the aim of the proposed Strategic Arms Reduction Talks (START).

It was pointed out that the types of weapons that are to be kept are the most modern multiple-warhead missiles, which would enable either side to deliver a crippling first strike.[3] The ability to do this is doubly destabilizing: a first strike may be a tempting way to end the cold war for all time with relatively little response. The knowledge of the opponent's capability to do so will put both sides on edge. In times of crisis, this knowledge would generate mounting additional tension that one side may eventually relieve by unleashing its first strike, simply because it becomes convinced that the other side is about to do the same. It would be a replay of the *Vincennes* syndrome on a gigantic scale.

Since such action must aim to cripple the opponent's retaliatory forces in one blow, it must be massive. All missile silos, command centers, nuclear weapons depots, bases for long-range bombers, and submarine bases would become targets. It would require 3,000 warheads with a total yield equivalent to 1,300 megatons of TNT, all well within the capabilities of each side, even after the proposed 50 percent reduction of ICBMs. The civilian fatalities resulting from such a *counterforce attack* on the United States are estimated as between twelve and twenty-seven million people, roughly the same as in an all-out attack on major population centers.[3] This has to do with the fact that many military targets are near large cities, and large-scale firestorms, together with widespread radioactive fallout, are to be expected.

If present and contemplated arms reductions are largely cosmetic, and with the Star Wars concept an expensive dream, how and when can we hope to remove this instability that keeps Drake's seventh term so dangerously low? A near-total nuclear disarmament appears to be the only hope. The goal is easily stated but not as easily achieved. There must be, of course, on both sides the strong desire to do it. In the hawkish climate that still pervades much of the relations between the superpowers, there seems to be little enthusiasm for such a course. The sentiment on our side is still that only a fool would disarm. Similar sentiments undoubtedly exist on the other side.

I don't want to belittle the problems or the risks. The transition from nuclear to conventional defenses has its own pitfalls. And when we have safely reached a nuclear-free world, being sure that no missiles are tucked away in some well-hidden silos in Siberia (or Utah), we will have gained a level of security no better than what existed prior to World War II, with major conflicts no longer holding the specter of total annihilation, and therefore again more likely to be entered.

We cannot, of course, destroy the technical know-how to build nuclear weapons anew, and we may assume that in a major conflict with conventional weapons, either side would resort to that alternative rather than face military defeat. But it is doubtful that an arsenal of total annihilation, involving thousands of nuclear warheads and their delivery systems, could be constructed in the course of an all-out war. The losses would again be immense, but civilization would be likely to survive.

The gains of total nuclear disarmament may seem modest. But having accomplished this gigantic cooperative venture might promote enough mutual trust to face together the other problems that are equally menacing.

The Population Bomb

It has been called that because the growth of the world population in this century has been spectacular. The future growth, if the trends continue, can only be described as explosive.

The most severe threats to civilization are derived from this single fact. They include massive pollution of the atmosphere and water supplies by our wastes, inadequate food supplies, escalating urbanization, progressive overcrowding, and inevitable fights for resources and living space.

The changes we have observed in only a few decades are frightening. I remember my first visit to São Paulo, when as a young man I lived in Brazil. The city was reached in a spectacular train ride that took the traveler from the port of Santos to the three-thousand-foot-high plateau on which São Paulo is located. After the steaming tropical heat of Santos, São Paulo seemed a paradise. With its large parks, wide esplanades lined with shade trees, clear air, and moderate climate, it was then the Brazilian city most cherished by affluent Europeans.

São Paulo is now, some fifty years later, one of the most congested, polluted, and still fastest growing cities in the world. A contemporary Brazilian novelist, Ignacio de Loyola Brandão, draws this nightmare picture of São Paulo in the year 2000, with the city having reached a population of twenty-six million:

> They say they've tried everything to get rid of the constant, nauseating odor of death and decomposition. . . . Bodies pile up waiting to be cremated. Open-air sewers disgorge their contents into old riverbeds. . . . The haze seems to be getting lower by the day. . . . The air trapped underneath, inflamed, is unbearable.[4]

The vision is grim, but not unrealistic. To appreciate the severity of the population explosion we must understand the nature of exponential growth. A simple example will illustrate: Let us say a kind uncle invested one dollar in your name on your date of birth at a fixed interest rate of 7 percent. On your first birthday you would have $1.07. During your second year your capital would earn 7 percent of $1.07, still only seven cents. In the third year your compound interest would jump to eight cents; you would have $1.22 on your third birthday. At this rate it will take ten years to double the original investment. You'll have four dollars at age twenty, eight at age thirty.

By now you have forgotten about your uncle's slowly growing legacy. In fact, the investment is overlooked by your children and grandchildren and is rediscovered only two hundred years after your birth by your great-great-great-great-grandson, who suddenly finds he has inherited a one-million-dollar windfall.

The earth's population has not always grown exponentially, that is, like capital invested at a fixed rate of return. We don't have exact numbers for the past, but we know that it had taken all of human history up to the year 1800 before the population reached one billion. Only about a hundred years later it had doubled to two billion. The four billion mark was reached in 1974, five billion in 1987. The present growth rate is 1.7 percent per year, which gives a doubling time of just forty years.

The frightening aspect of these figures is that the world's population has lately been growing faster than exponentially, as expressed by the famous doomsday equation. But even if the growth rate were held constant at its present value, there would be over six billion people on earth in the year 2000, thirty-four billion in A.D. 2100, and thirty trillion in A.D. 2500. If all this humanity were spread evenly over the entire landmass of the earth, there would then be one human for every twenty square feet of ground. By the end of the third millennium every square inch of land and sea would be covered to a height of several hundred feet with human bodies.

Enough! It isn't going to happen. The only question is, What will prevent it? The three horsemen, war, famine, and pestilence, can always be relied on to step in if needed. But we should be able to do better than that. If only we understand clearly what is happening, we should have little difficulty stabilizing the population at a reasonable level. The process of procreation is, after all, something we all understand.

The Greenhouse Effect

In the early summer of 1988, which turned out to be unusually warm over most of the United States, James Hansen of NASA's Goddard Institute for Space Studies made a startling announcement in testimony before a Senate subcommittee: "The greenhouse effect has been detected and is changing our climate now," he stated with "99 percent confidence."

What is the greenhouse effect? The atmosphere extends a blanket around the earth that allows the beneficial radiation of the sun to reach the earth's surface but blocks most of the ultraviolet and infrared. The warm earth, in turn, reradiates some of this energy, a fraction of which escapes back into space. But the remainder stays trapped within the atmosphere, warming our blanket.

The temperature of the earth depends critically on the fraction of the earth's reradiated heat that can penetrate the atmosphere and escape. If more of it were trapped, the temperature would rise. That is the greenhouse effect. If more radiation were allowed to escape into space, the earth would get colder.

The amount of heat radiation stopped within the atmosphere depends on the presence of the so-called greenhouse gases, chiefly carbon dioxide, methane, and nitrous oxide. These all occur naturally in the upper atmosphere. Without them virtually all heat radiated by the surface of the earth would escape, and drastic cooling would result. Eventually the entire earth would be covered by a layer of ice. Scientists now believe that the climatic swings between the ice ages and the warm interglacial epochs of the Pleistocene were the result of relatively minor changes in the concentration of carbon dioxide.

But much larger changes in the concentration of greenhouse gases have resulted from escalating industrialization since the middle of the nineteenth century. Carbon dioxide concentration has risen from 275 parts per million by volume in 1850 to 345 in 1985 and continues to rise at close to 5 percent in every decade. Something like five billion tons of carbon are being sent into the atmosphere annually, as a result of the burning of fossil fuels.

The systematic burning of tropical rain forests adds significantly to the load of greenhouse gases dispatched annually into our stratosphere. For the most part, poor farmers in the Brazilian Amazon basin burn small parcels of rain forest, from which they earn meager crops for a few years until the thin soil turns to dust. They are then forced to continue the process. Similar destruction is going on in West Africa. The loss of the world's rain forests is doubly damaging because of the massive pollution it sends into the atmosphere and because forests are natural absorbers of carbon dioxide, returning oxygen back into the atmosphere.

The concentrations of the other natural greenhouse gases, methane and nitrous oxide, have also increased significantly as a result of industrialization. To these are now added the chlorofluorocarbons (CFCs), synthetic gases that have been widely used in industry and are also powerful absorbers of infrared. It is estimated that a molecule of CFCs is ten thousand times more effective in absorbing infrared than one of carbon dioxide. CFCs have the additional effect of destroying the stratospheric ozone layer that protects life from ultraviolet radiation.[5]

Long-term effects of these changes are a matter of profound worry among atmospheric scientists. Continued increase in greenhouse gas emissions will almost certainly cause pronounced warming over the next decades, whether or not one agrees with Hansen's statement that the greenhouse effect has already arrived. The effects of global warming could be devastating. We can expect an increase in the number and severity of hurricanes and droughts, and extensive flooding of low-lying coastal areas resulting from the melting of polar glaciers. These effects are expected during the early part of the twenty-first century.

"If we went all out to slow the warming trend, we might stall sea-level rise at three to six feet," according to Robert Buddemeier, an environmental scientist at Lawrence Livermore National Laboratory. The worldwide effect of a six-foot rise would include flooding of many islands in the Pacific, the Indian Ocean, and the Caribbean, causing "a refugee problem of unprecedented proportions."[6]

Coastal cities such as New York, Boston, Miami, New Orleans, Galveston would have to be protected by dams. Some would have to be abandoned. The loss of arable land, particularly on the Indian subcontinent, would have catastrophic consequences.

Once set into motion, the greenhouse effect cannot be readily arrested or reversed. Our civilization runs largely on fossil fuels. Replacements are hard to come by, and radical changes are fraught with technological difficulties.

Many of the consequences mentioned take years, even decades, to develop, and we are left with the dilemma of either making drastic decisions now, anticipating the worst (and perhaps overreacting, as some would see it), or waiting for more information, a better understanding of the intricate dynamics of the processes (and perhaps missing our chance of saving the planet).

The choices are far from clear-cut. Remedies for perceived hazards carry risks of their own. Should we, for instance, curtail now the burning of fossil fuels and have nuclear power fill the energy gap, or would that be acting hastily? We have here another example of the weakening link between our runaway technology and the human ability to manage the control room. In a giant *Stark-Vincennes* syndrome in slow motion, we are caught between the specters of the skipper of the *USS Stark,* who waited too long and took a missile from an Iraqi fighter plane, and the captain of the *Vincennes,* who acted too soon and downed an airbus.

Meanwhile, the theory of the greenhouse effect is being confirmed by what has been called "an inadvertent global experiment" which amounts to continuing to do what we have been doing all along.[5]

There have been some modest attempts to act. Some energy-conserving policies were instituted in the United States a few years ago, mainly in response to the energy crisis resulting from the oil embargo. Chlorofluorocarbons are no longer in general use as convenient propellants in spray cans, and some countries have banned most uses of CFCs. The United States now has an Environmental Protection Agency and a Clean Air Act. In 1987 the Montreal Protocol, signed by a few countries, was the first international agreement to limit the production of greenhouse gases, and in 1988 a manifesto issued by the International Conference on the Changing Atmosphere called for a 20 percent reduction in carbon dioxide emission by the year 2005, a shift to nonfossil energy sources, a halt in global deforestation, and total ban of the use of CFCs.

On the other hand, during the presidential election campaign of 1988, the environment was mentioned by both candidates in passing only. Unlike the lengthy discussions on the relative merits of the latest in weapons systems, no serious consideration was given to the urgent choices the new administration will have to face concerning the preservation of our fragile atmosphere, no agonizing thoughts on the environment have penetrated the consciousness of the American political process.

Pollution, Pollution, Pollution

A barrel of freshly squeezed grape juice forms a rich nutrient environment for a variety of microorganisms from bacteria to yeasts. Here they thrive and they multiply. Given the right temperature, there is a veritable population explosion of unicellular organisms feeding on the plentiful sugars and enzymes dissolved in the liquid. Soon there are waste products that accumulate and eventually turn life for these creatures from comfortable to precarious and from precarious to intolerable. Prominent among these is ethanol, or ethyl alcohol, the bacterial waste that eventually kills all the fauna in the barrel. Our miniature biosphere has turned to wine.

Pollution is the inevitable byproduct, and frequently the undoing, of a thriving colony of organisms. Our own barrel has been a rich provider; it has also been vast. On the scale of the Earth's virgin forests, its oceans and its atmosphere, human activities have until recently seemed puny and our needs insignificant compared with the potential resources of the planet.

This has been a costly delusion for some time. After a series of environmental disasters, such as massive sewage spills into the New York harbor and onto beaches of the New York area in 1988, Stephen

C. Joseph, the New York City Health Commissioner, said: "I do believe this period of the 1980s will be remembered as the time the planet struck back."

In the United States, the total amount of materials to be disposed of amounts to about twenty-five tons per person per year. Household waste is only a small portion of that mountain of junk; the rest is industrial waste, much of it toxic.

Waste has become a prime negative trading commodity. Poorer nations are bribed to accept the refuse of their more affluent contemporaries. According to a study by Greenpeace International, over three million tons of waste was sent from industrial to developing countries between 1986 and 1988. Six hundred thousand tons of toxic waste is transported yearly from West Germany to its poorer cousin, East Germany.

In 1987, the barge *Mobro* sailed out of New York harbor in search of a place to dump several thousand tons of waste from various Long Island communities. Like the legendary *Flying Dutchman*, the *Mobro* and its cargo were rejected in place after place of their five-thousand-mile journey. Since then, the new fleet of ghost ships has grown. In 1988, the *Deep Sea Carrier* and the *Karen B.*, laden with toxic wastes from Italy, sailed to Koko, Nigeria, in search of a landfill site. Nigeria didn't want the waste; neither did six European countries where the two ships vainly sought docking rights. Another vessel, the American *Khian Sea*, laden with twenty-eight million pounds of toxic ash from Philadelphia incinerators, sailed for two years without finding a friendly harbor. It was turned away from ports in the Bahamas, the Dominican Republic, Honduras, Costa Rica, and the Cape Verde Islands. It was later sighted passing through the Suez Canal under a new name, *Felicia*, apparently heading for the Indian Ocean and the Philippines. At last, the *Khian Sea*, alias *Felicia*, reappeared, empty. Its owners said the cargo was dumped, but they refused to say where.

On a smaller scale, here in the United States, a boxcar filled with radioactive waste was being shuttled between states, a *Flying Dutchman* on rails. Landfill sites have become scarce both in Europe and the United States, and the memory of Love Canal remains in the consciousness of every community.

Meanwhile, irresponsible haulers of all kinds of toxic wastes drop their cargo by the roadside, in rivers, or offshore. Thousands of drums of unwanted chemicals are slowly rusting and leaking in abandoned warehouses, empty lots, and fields.

Finding safe places to dispose of wastes is only part of the pollution problem. Runoff from farms and cities is heavy with pesticides, and with nitrogen from fertilizers and treated sewage, all flowing into rivers, estuaries, and coastal waters. Many of our sources of drinking water are affected.

In and around our cities, the air must absorb the emissions from industrial complexes and from millions of automobiles. The situation becomes critical on hot summer days, when atmospheric inversion layers reduce air circulation to a minimum. The resulting smog and high ozone content can make the air almost unbreathable.

Automobile emissions, together with sulphur dioxide from coal and oil-burning power plants, are responsible for the formation of nitric and sulphuric acid, which comes down as *acid rain.* Volker Mohnen, a professor of atmospheric science at the State University of New York at Albany, has called this "a large-scale interference in the biochemical cycles through which living things interact with their environment."[7]

Acid rain has many manifestations. It is likely to be responsible for extensive damage to forests in the United States and Europe. The dying of German forests, called *Waldsterben,* has been most dramatic. In the United States the damage is greatest in the East. More than 50 percent of the red spruce has died within the past twenty-five years in parts of New York, Vermont, and New Hampshire.

While the link between acid rain and forest loss is still circumstantial, there is no question about the devastating effect acid rain has had on the ecology of our lakes. A National Surface Water Survey reported that 10 percent of the lakes in Michigan's upper peninsula and 11 percent of the lakes in New York's Adirondacks had exhausted their acid-neutralizing capacity. Life in these lakes has been drastically altered or totally abolished.

Intelligent choices that must be made today often depend on our ability to project far into the future. This is especially true for the most stubborn of pollution problems, the disposal of radioactive wastes from nuclear power plants and weapons laboratories. Some fifteen thousand tons of highly radioactive waste are now held in temporary storage at locations all over the country. These facilities are rapidly approaching saturation. By the year 2000, some fifty thousand tons of radioactive material will have to be disposed of.

Radioactivity cannot be deactivated. The best we can do is store the material in a safe place until it has decayed. That process may take seconds or millennia, depending on the chemical element. The by-products of nuclear fission, such as the spent uranium fuel rods, are a mix of elements of widely differing half-lives and will remain dangerously radioactive for some ten thousand years.

Present plans are for permanent storage of all radioactive waste deep underground in a location that ensures a stable environment. The most promising site is Nevada's Yucca Mountain. Plans are to construct a cavity about a thousand feet below the surface, to hold up to seventy thousand tons of radioactive waste in sealed canisters. The site is chosen for its outstanding geological stability, the scarcity of rainfall in the area, and the low water table.

The facility could be opened by the year 2003 and would be filled to capacity and sealed by 2030. The canisters, using the best available technology, should remain intact for centuries, but are likely to start disintegrating within a thousand years. If the water table remains as it is now, safely below the level of the intended storage, even ruptured canisters will not cause contamination to be carried outside the sealed storage area. There are other *ifs*. We must assume that the climate will not change drastically in the next ten thousand years, that no major earthquakes will rock the area, and that no future generation will inadvertently open up the deadly enclosure.[8]

What is the life expectancy of a technological civilization? We have no statistics on which to base an answer, being the only technological civilization anyone has ever known. As things stand, our future is as uncertain as the roll of perfect billiard balls after ten collisions in the example in chapter five. We have become powerful beyond all expectations, only to find ourselves threatened by our own toys of war, as well as by our instruments of peace. Our present decisions reach out farther into the future than anything mankind has done in the past, but the outcome is uncertain. There was a time when our visions were centuries ahead of reality. It was humanity's dream time. We now have difficulty grasping the terrible impact of the present.

This has been a disheartening chapter to write. Science began when humans had the audacity to pit their brain power against every mystery with which nature confronted them. One after another, the mysteries have yielded to our supreme self-confidence and steady pursuit. Perhaps we were not prepared to be challenged now by a problem as mundane as the human threat to human existence. A few years ago, I was advising a female college student on her academic curriculum. She wanted to major in sanitary engineering. "Why do you want to do that?" I asked at one point. The cryptosexist remark was a disguise for, "Why would a good-looking girl like you want to study sludge?" Her answer was one of mild surprise and reproach. "Don't you think it's important?" she asked. The gut reaction remains. The study of pollution does not seem like science in the grand tradition of the Greeks. But the problem has grown to such compelling proportions that it merits the best minds, the most heroic efforts. Nobel prizes, or their equivalents, should be awarded to anyone who can devise new ways of dealing with the burgeoning load of our waste.[9]

CHAPTER X

Perspectives

LANGUAGE, SCIENCE, ART, the noble aspects of our history as well as the shady ones, our weary outlook on the future — they all come together in and emanate from that unique function of the human brain we call *mind*. It is the most powerful mover of our destinies, and yet, we have difficulty demonstrating that it even exists. Leibnitz gave that striking description of our vain attempts to find *ourselves:* "A man goes out of his house, looks in at the window, and is surprised to find that the room is empty."

How, then, are we to find our way? Who, or what will be our guide? But the empty room, to continue Leibnitz's metaphor, springs to life with a single occupant, who — merely by thinking — creates around himself a universe seething with activity. This has been called *circular causality* (see Wiener's definition on p. 96), *self-transcendence, the Promethean gene,* or just *consciousness.* It describes the power to *reflect, resolve,* and *create.*

"Existence conditions consciousness," said Karl Marx, to which Joseph Brodsky, the Russian poet, essayist, and winner of the Nobel prize for literature in 1987, replied that this "was true only for as long as it takes consciousness to acquire the art of estrangement; thereafter, consciousness is on its own and can both condition and ignore existence."[1]

Both statements are terse, especially when taken out of context. We understand Marx's preoccupation with the powerful grip the environment (existence) exerts on human affairs (consciousness). But what does Brodsky mean by "the art of estrangement"? It seems an odd expression when applied to consciousness, since consciousness is generally taken to be a kind of passive familiarity not only with the world around us but with ourselves. Brodsky reminds us that consciousness is a *source* of reality, not just its observer, and that self-consciousness is not only to know oneself, but to *make* oneself.

We are not compelled to base our actions on the mores, customs, or other dictates of our culture, nor on evolutionary selections that, eons ago, provided us with some adaptive advantage. We have argued too long about the relative weights of nature and nurture, as though we had to be slaves to one or the other. I believe that is what Brodsky meant when he said that "consciousness is on its own."

Resolutions arise from the realization of the absurdity of some of our ways, the incongruity between our actions and our needs. Such realizations don't come easily, but are often gleaned — as in a mirror — in a story or in a work of art. The impact of Shirley Jackson's short story "The Lottery" has to do with the familiarity, the downright folksiness of its characters, which contrasts with their savage custom of stoning to death one of their members in an atmosphere resembling a country fair. By contrast, the violence depicted in the magnificent Assyrian sculptures that lined the palace walls at Nineveh and Nimrud is generally regarded as belonging to a bloodthirsty but long-forgotten past. But the incongruity in Jackson's story stands out only because the characters are homey and the custom is unfamiliar. How many savageries do we overlook because they are part of our own civilization's heritage?

The Violent Hominid

It is difficult to reject the notion that violence is in our genes. There are too many examples of mayhem inflicted by humans on one another to believe that it is all culturally conditioned. Cultures differ widely, but time and again we are shocked to find brutality and murder among what we took to be the gentlest of peoples. This is true for the Samoans, so lovingly and trustingly portrayed by Margaret Mead, as well as for the !Kung bushmen, the so-called harmless people, of the Kalahari desert. Both of these have now been shown to have a high incidence of violent crime.

The Gebusi, a small tribe living in the New Guinea rain forest, have been described as "a strikingly gentle lot," except for the fact that "behind this aura of serenity . . . the Gebusi murder one another at a rate among the highest ever reported. . . ."[2]

Unlike the Samoans, !Kung, and Gebusi, the Yanomamo tribe of Amazon Indians has a reputation of being a fierce, warlike society, in which tribal warfare and retaliatory murder alternate in bloody succession. To have killed somebody appears to be a status symbol among Yanomamo males, and anthropologists report that this distinction confers upon the killer the advantages of more wives and more numerous offspring.[3]

Chimpanzees, our nearest relatives in the animal kingdom, who long enjoyed the reputation of gentle herbivores, were observed to kill their own kind in occasional forays, much to the dismay of their most dedicated chronicler, Jane Goodall.

Western civilization has taught us to shun the more blatant aspects of homicide. I recall a short story I read long ago, probably in German. It was set somewhere in the Polish countryside, sometime in the last century, when Polish freedom fighters were carrying on a prolonged struggle against Russian domination.

It was a time when soldiers wore ragged but colorful uniforms in the field of battle and when officers were handsome, had mustaches, rode into battle on horseback, and carried sabers as tokens of their manhood and authority.

The story opens when a group of Polish partisans have captured some Russian officers, lined them up against the trees at the edge of a small clearing, and are about to shoot them. The proceedings are held up temporarily when one of the Poles points out that they could use the fine shirts, the tunics, and the boots the Russians are wearing, and wouldn't it be a shame to pump them full of bullet holes.

It is agreed. The prisoners are told to strip off their clothes, and the firing squad resume positions. Again there is a delay. Firing upon a group of shivering, naked men does not seem to be part of the mystique of fighting a war of liberation. Again the muskets are lowered, and the prisoners are told to get dressed again. With the uniforms hiding the Russians' bodies, the Poles have no trouble completing what they have set out to do. This was not murder, it was simply part of the war, and the blood of the executed complemented in proper fashion the colorful tunics and the fine white shirts they wore below.

We generally exhibit a noble reluctance to inflict harm on others who, like the naked Russian prisoners, have no visible mark to set them apart from ourselves, though the story has a hollow ring when we think of the millions of Jews marched naked to their doom in German gas chambers.

But in our more civilized acts of violence we like our victims clothed, if not in uniforms at least in ideas or symbols. A strange religion can bring out our most feral passions. Nothing is as likely to incite hostility as somebody's belief in a God with whom we are not on speaking terms. No activity seems so distasteful as a ritual that does not evoke childhood memories in us. Ecumenism aside, and the many nice things American clergymen say about one another from their respective pulpits, the ongoing slaughter between Hindus and Sikhs in India, the blind hatred between Protestants and Catholics in Northern Ireland, and the savagery of total war between all shades of religion in the Middle East are testimony to the mindless rage brought about by conflicting deities.

Why do we do it? Many possible roots of violence have been cited, fear, frustration, social conditioning, and genetic disposition among them. Part of the old Adam we have not yet been able to transcend. These are probably all valid. There is also self-righteousness, and its cousin, *loyalty*. In listing loyalty among the culprits, I realize I am attacking a sacred cow. To be loyal is a noble attribute most of us aspire to. Loyalty is affection, gratitude, self-sacrifice. But loyalty is also often seen as an obligation to tilt one's judgment, curb one's nagging doubts, and to rally unquestioningly behind an idea, slogan, or symbol. Such loyalty, which is a vestige of pre-Darwinian *essentialism*, tends to promote moral blindness, self-righteousness, and violence.

It may still be an adaptive advantage among the Yanomamo Indians, but in most societies today, the tendency to commit violence is more likely to land you in jail. On an international scale, unfortunately — although appropriate moral standards are universally agreed upon in principle — we lack independent juries to establish guilt, and, anyway, countries can heed or reject the verdicts of international courts at their discretion. Given the proper manipulation of their own populace, most governments find it relatively easy to garner the necessary internal support for almost any action.

But here, also, we find that aggressiveness is even less advantageous than it used to be, and — given the built-in instability of the world balanced on the knife-edge of mutual assured destruction — may ultimately be catastrophic. Goethe was wrong when he said that our hidden urges generally point us in the right direction. It seems that our collective gene pool and societal interactions cannot be trusted. The voices within us, and those around us, often speak an ancient language, befitting a different time. We must counter with a watchful consciousness that practices the "art of estrangement," and if necessary forego the comfort of loyalty. At any rate, finding the right way, rather than being instinctual, will often require intellectual efforts of the most strenuous kind, without which our sociobiological system will surely self-destruct.

What I am suggesting raises, of course, the most complex ethical issues. Our society is founded on laws, most of which are designed to make our world better and fairer. Violations bring punishments, as they should. But laws can become obsolete, and situations arise that would make compliance seem less ethical than violation. On occasion we are required to participate in, or at least condone, actions that violate our own sense of right and wrong. If we now said that everyone should follow the dictates of his or her own moral judgment, we would invite lawlessness and chaos, while rigid adherence to all laws and moral standards of the society would make individual ethics superfluous. We come up against a situation here in which no advice can be given. With all the laws and standards that society has set up, the individual is ultimately and unequivocally on his own.

The Human Family

In chapter III we talked about the manner in which *Homo sapiens* diverged from its predecessor, *Homo erectus*. Human beings, it turns out, are an unusually homogeneous species. Genetic studies suggest that modern man emerged in a single location in Africa and spread from there over the rest of the world.

But just as remarkable as our genetic uniformity is the great diversity of the human spirit. It sems to come from out of nowhere. Place that rigid framework of human genes into an environment — any environment — and it will sprout ideas and behavior that are always fresh and mostly unpredictable, like the fire scattered in all directions by the monotonous lattice of carbon atoms in a gem-cut diamond that is held up to light. This is admittedly a weak metaphor for the emergence of mind in the interplay of nature and nurture.

We have invented for ourselves such diverse goals as becoming artists, scientists, airline pilots, and Zen priests; we fill every niche of political opinions; and we subscribe to every possible belief system in what Brodsky termed *consciousness conditioning* and *ignoring existence*. We ignore existence, the limitations of existence, that is, when we seek out physical hardships for which our bodies are ill-equipped, or strive for intellectual achievements never envisioned by evolution. We also ignore the intimate relatedness of all humans, when we look for and amplify the minutest distinctions among us, until we find ourselves surrounded by what looks more like our natural enemies than members of our own close-knit species.

There is a reason for this. Our intellect has great difficulty dealing with unity, because, without a background against which to measure our ideas and ourselves, we have no yardstick. Without opposing forces, our efforts seem to fall into a vacuum. We do our best creative thinking in adversity and in interaction with an adversary. An interesting parallel exists in physics. Time and space are meaningful references when we are dealing with a portion of the universe — objects on earth, a star, or even a galaxy. But when we contemplate the universe as a whole we have lost all signposts. Questions such as, Where does it come from? and Where is it going? become meaningless.[4]

In antiquity the Greeks coined the phrase "Man is the measure of all things." To the Athenians, "man" meant Athenian, not Spartan, and certainly not barbarian. Today, we are still applying the standard in the same parochial manner, as though substituting *mankind* for *man* would plunge us into an existential and moral vacuum.

But very recent history has brought profound changes that we are just beginning to recognize. Our environment has been up to now a virtually limitless stage on which to display our varied plumage and play our games of war and peace. It is only in the last few decades that the walls have moved in on us, and we perceive forces that are equally hostile to all of us: the dwindling resources, our own explosive population growth, the deterioration of our atmosphere and our waters, the dramatic accumulation of our wastes with no place to put them, and a technology of mass annihilation whose hair-trigger control strains our nerves and threatens our existence.

These new hostile forces provide us with a novel frame of reference, and allow us, compel us, for the first time in our history, to view humanity as *one,* because, for the first time every action we take against one another will be to our own detriment. This is not an easy lesson to learn. We still react to the nuclear threat by trying to build a Super Excalibur, that now discredited centerpiece of the Star Wars effort. It is a comic strip mentality unworthy of the doubly wise. Still, our enmities are deep, our genes are combative, and prejudice is a disease of the mind humans are heir to. We must expose it and treat it with understanding, instead of answering it in kind. If that is what Christ meant by "turning the other cheek," the admonition was premature, by two millennia.

The Mind and the Machine

If not doing what is rational is a sign of faulty thinking, how do we think properly? From many examples in this book it appears that our brains are burdened with a sociobiological albatross that deflects rational thought. Must we then cultivate an emotionless, more computerlike function of the brain?

It will certainly be necessary to strengthen our ability to select from the many possible scenarios the most beneficial path. This will require enormous intellectual effort. Fortunately, we have at our disposal an arsenal of computers and supercomputers with their vast memory and computational power. We have only begun to make full use of them. In the field of medicine, for example, diagnosis and therapy selection could be improved greatly if every physician had at his or her disposal an up-to-date profile of pathologies and complete statistics on success and failure rates of medications and surgical procedures. Such *global* strategies, drawing on probabilities computed from a worldwide data base, are already used extensively in weather forecasting. This may seem like a return to what was labeled in chapter II an essentialist or collectivist approach that led to abuses like the eugenics movement. Many physicians argue, with some justification, that no machine can substitute for the personal knowledge he may have of the patient. But often, individual judgment is inadequate and statistical information becomes valuable. In the Center for Disease Control in Atlanta, Georgia, computers are able to spot trends in pathologies and relate them to outbreaks of communicable diseases or the result of new products that have come into use.

We may look forward to increasing reliance on computers in all kinds of decision making, in place of intuition, instinct, or judgments based on custom or emotions. This will mean a check on some of our so-called better instincts like compassion, which may seem a high price to pay. But compassion is a capricious virtue. The Palestinian elicits little compassion from the Israeli settler and vice versa. Compassion can become infectious, as when a whole nation anxiously followed the fate of two whales trapped in arctic ice, or it can vanish without a trace when one ethnic group slaughters another "for a cause."

Are we then bound to become automata, with our brains restricted to feeding information into the data banks of our computers and receiving from them our instructions? Is the ultimate irony of our search for artificial intelligence that we are becoming more like machines?

There is no denying that some freedoms will have to be sacrificed. One of these is the unrestrained pursuit of knowledge, as I have pointed out in chapter VII. But, I do not see computers as anything but our obedient servants in tasks where the human brain is slow and clumsy, as in recalling lists and manipulating large numbers. I recall traveling in the Soviet Union some years ago and finding long lines at airport ticket counters awaiting the arrival *by air* of handwritten ledgers containing passenger lists and reservations. I tell this story whenever someone laments the increasing automation in our lives. I do not foresee a takeover by computers. If the brain is poor at computing, it is the brain that has thought of arithmetic algorithms to do with pencil and paper what it can't do in the head, and eventually invented computers. By comparison, a computer, which is poor in inventiveness, does not analyze the rules of creativity and will not construct a brain.

The advocates of "hard AI" like to point out that any mental task that is understood can, in principle, be done by a computer. This is the "you-define-it-and-we'll-put-it-in" challenge. I would like to counter that with "*you* define it and I'll put it in myself." But creativity defies the kind of definition that could be useful for such purposes. Human consciousness is still the least predictable system in all of the known universe. In fashioning its *creative loops,* it is able to reach beyond its own biological limitations, just as it did when it invented the first stone tool. Reason will compel us to follow the rational deductions reached by our logical machines, but the knowledge gained will only expand the horizons of the human mind. And it will be the minds of *individual* humans that will continue to create the future visions in science, in art, and in new concepts of human coexistence. We turn once more to the words of Brodsky, who found a poet's way of expressing the old Darwinian truth that collective nouns are "approximations, conventions, common denominators, and that numerators are what civilization is all about."[5]

Of Death and Renewal

There is danger in allowing our consciousness to soar without constraint and go too far "ignoring existence." Humans alone in the animal kingdom have the capacity to will their own destruction or at least to rationalize their doom. Soldiers by the millions have marched willingly to their deaths, statesmen have proclaimed their willingness to die for an idea, and religious fanatics of all ages have submitted themselves to torture and death for an extravagance of mind called faith.

Suicide is the ultimate estrangement, and humans have perfected this art individually and collectively from Cleopatra to Hemingway, from Masada to Jonestown.

The unique bent to "let go," to "throw in the sponge," has a universal counterpart in religious millennialism, which in various forms asserts that we have reached "the end of the tether" and should now accept the inevitable. The "inevitable" is a form of Armageddon, that is, the end of the world as we know it and the beginning of a phase that has terrible consequences for the sinner but is not too bad for a few blessed souls.

Such sentiments were widespread before the year A.D. 1000 and then again in the early nineteenth century, especially in the northeastern part of the United States, where William Miller founded the *Millerite* movement and predicted that the Second Coming of Christ would occur sometime between March 1843 and March 1844. Michael Barkun, a professor of political science at Syracuse University, has studied these movements and points to the similarity between the apocalyptic cults of the last century and some of today's fundamentalist doctrines.[6] I mentioned in chapter I the Reverend Royce Elms of Amarillo, Texas, and his prediction of the end of the world by 1990.

Sentiments of doom, according to Barkun, usually arise in the wake of disasters. At a certain point, the mind tires of having to deal with seemingly hopeless situations. Barkun sees "a veil of pessimism surrounding the year 2000."

But, at the bottom of every apocalyptic view there is a sense of fulfillment and of renewal. The fulfillment is religious mysticism, but the renewal is undoubtedly taken from the example of nature. We see renewal after such catastrophes as forest fires or volcanic devastations like the eruption of Mount Saint Helens, a few years back. New life crowds soon into the sterile residue, often more vigorous and more prolific than that which was destroyed. After the extensive forest fires that ravaged Yellowstone National Park in 1988, the cones of the lodgepole pines that had lain in the ground for years, their scales sealed shut by hardened resin, popped open, and their seeds soon sprouted in the still warm earth. The global catastrophe sixty-five million years ago that triggered the massive extinction of most species of the Cretaceous period, dinosaurs among them, made possible the rise of mammals and the eventual evolution of hominids. Evolution itself is a story of death and renewal, since selection of the successful is contingent on the demise of the less fortunate, and every mutation is an accident that is potentially lethal.

But all that is hindsight. It would be folly to invite catastrophes in the anticipation that better things may arise from the ashes, or to expose ourselves purposely to radiation in the hope of causing favorable mutations. It is wise to accept disasters after the fact and to make the best of whatever benefits they may bring with them. But we must never invite disasters out of despair. Hope is our most useful commodity, and we must fight for our existence with all the means our civilization has at its disposal and with all the sapience after which this species was named.

Our challenge will be to structure society, on a global scale, so that law is justly projected downward through the hierarchy of its institutions. At the same time — and that is the greater challenge — any such system must wither unless the creative ideas of individuals (the only source of creative ideas) are allowed to percolate freely upward to modify the collective wisdom.

If a "veil of pessimism" still clouds humanity's future, there are at last hints that the veil may be lifting, and that, with a greater awareness of the magnitude of global threats, has come a new confidence in our ability to deal with them.

Concern for the environment has deepened and spread over wider areas of the political spectrum. The feeling is slowly growing, also, that wars have become as anachronistic as our ancient, genetically conditioned craving for fat.

The cold war between the superpowers may be over, as was announced by British Prime Minister Margaret Thatcher in 1988, but it is not the end of hatred, prejudice, and bloody conflicts. Although I am more optimistic now than I was two years ago, when I began writing this book, I see some of the old global problems being replaced by new ones. Perhaps the nuclear standoff is less of an imminent threat today, but the profusion of weapons technology among the so-called third world nations is confronting us with a situation in which, sooner or later, *everybody* will be in a position to inflict intolerable damage on everybody else, by long-range missiles tipped with chemical or biological, if not nuclear, warheads. The superpowers may be able to forestall this for a while, but not for long. The military edge high technology confers on its creators is but a temporary reprieve. The experience with the atom bomb taught us that knowledge of any kind cannot be bottled up for long in any one segment of our sociable species. Eventually it becomes the great equalizer.

The universal ability to do great harm to other nations will increase dramatically in the future, and deterrence, while effective up to a point, breaks down when anger or misguided apocalyptic thinking or technological breakdown turns us suicidal. But it is not deterrence that keeps most of us from killing each other in the street but the lack of desire to kill, coupled with a measure of confidence in the mechanisms society has devised to keep us all alive and well. These lessons have not yet been applied on a global scale.

This has been a wrenching century, with the memorials to our madness more numerous and more poignant than the record of our many magnificent achievements. There could be ample cause for despair, for "abandoning ourselves to Providence." But despair can always wait. Let the apocalypse come when our sun dies a few billion years hence or when the universe ends in the big crunch many billions of years after that. For now, let us resolve to keep alive and cultivate the spark of the human mind on this crowded but still beautiful planet.

Notes

INTRODUCTION

1. "Man," "mankind" will be used in the sense of the German *Mensch,* together with "human being," or "human," to refer to the species or to a member of the species *Homo sapiens,* with no gender connotation intended.

2. Dyson (1988), p. 110.

3. Melvin Konner, "What Our Ancestors Ate," *New York Times Magazine,* June 5, 1988.

4. Nietzsche, in Kaufmann (1954), p. 50.

CHAPTER I

1. Alexander Marshak, an archaeologist and researcher at the Peabody Museum at Harvard University, describes this find in an article ("Reading Before Writing," *New York Times Book Review,* April 6, 1986) and similar cases of apparent record-keeping in a book (Marshak, 1972).

2. The number 36,000 is traced to Sumerian mathematics based on powers of 60. The fourth power of 60 is 12,960,000. The year was taken as 360 days (6 × 60). Thus 12,960,000 days is 36,000 years, which is the Great Year, also called Babylonian Year or Platonic Year. See, for example, Sarton (1952), pp. 71, 119.

3. Cohn (1961), p. 35.

4. For a discussion of the profound changes brought about by the transition from a steady state philosophy to that of evolving species, see, for example, Mayr (1982), p. 303.

5. Lopez (1964), p. 2.

6. Lopez (1964), p. 27.

7. The quotation about Vinland is attributed to Adam of Bremen (c. 1070) and appears in Lopez (1964), p. 19.

8. Several versions of Urban's speech are extant. This one is reported by F. Ogg, quoted by Durant (1950), p. 587.

9. The description of the First Crusade follows the account given by Cohn (1961).

10. The story of the Crusaders at Caesarea and the quotations are from Daniel (1975), p. 116.

11. Cohn (1961), p. 68.

12. Durant (1950), p. 592.

13. Daniel (1975), p. 121.

14. The spirit of Amarillo has recently been described by Grace Mojtabai (1986) in her book *Blessed Assurance: At Home with the Bomb in Amarillo, Texas.*

15. From an article by Robert Reinhold, "Curious Author Has Come to

Accept City in Texas that Accepts the Bomb," *New York Times,* September 15, 1986.

1. These opinions were expressed at an international workshop of population geneticists and paleobiologists held in West Berlin in June 1985. (See report by Roger Lewin, *Science* 229: 23–24, 1985.)

2. Mayr (1984).

3. For a good discussion of the development of evolutionary ideas since Darwin, see, for example, E. Mayr (1982), pp. 479–627.

4. The theory of genetic drift is chiefly the work of the American evolutionary theorist Sewall Wright. Provine (1986) has recently published an account of Wright and his work.

5. Lewontin (1984).

6. Mayr (1982), p. 589.

7. The theory of punctuated equilibria was first proposed by Eldredge and Gould (1972). For a brief discussion on gradualism vs. saltatory evolution, see Mayr (1982), p. 617.

8. An excellent discussion of the abuse of so-called measurements of mental characteristics is found in Gould (1981).

9. A richly illustrated summary of early hominid fossils and reconstructions and an account of the Laetoli footprints appeared in the November 1985 issue of *National Geographic;* see articles by Kenneth F. Weaver, "The Search for Our Ancestors," and by Richard Leakey and Alan Walker, "*Homo erectus* Unearthed." See also Washburn and Moore (1977).

10. Walter M. Bortz II, "Physical Exercise as an Evolutionary Force," *Journal of Human Evolution* 14: 145–155, 1985.

11. Wendt (1972), p. 256. For a recent summary of chimpanzee research see also the excellent illustrated account by Goodall (1986).

12. This point is made by Jared Diamond, "Making a Chimp Out of Man," *Discover,* December 1984.

13. There is considerable controversy over whether the successful learning of a series of sign-language signals, apparently mastered by several chimpanzees and gorillas, constitutes a true linguistic ability. In one view, Diamond (see note 12) predicts that the vocalizations of wild apes will be found to contain elements of a language.

14. Konrad Lorenz's quotation is taken from Wendt (1972), p. 254.

15. The DNA studies on apes and man were carried out by Charles Sibley and Jon Ahlquist. The account is taken from Diamond (see note 12).

16. Roger Lewin, "The Origin of the Modern Human Mind," *Science* 236: 668–670, 1987. Report on a meeting of anthropologists in Cambridge, England.

17. The relatively recent discovery of this remarkable fossil skeleton, the Boy of Nariokotome, was described in an article by Pat Shipman, "When Skeletons Speak," *Discover,* April 1986.

18. I am referring here to the processes of *reflection* and *self-reference*

which I have discussed in greater detail in *Windows on the Mind* (Harth, 1982).

CHAPTER III

1. This was pointed out, for example, in S. J. Gould and R. C. Lewontin's article "The Spandrels of San Marco and the Panglossian Paradigm: A Critique of the Adaptionist Programme," *Proceedings Royal Society, London*, B, 205, 1984; also Gould and Lewontin (1984).

2. The theory of *gene-culture coevolution* was first presented by Lumsden and Wilson (1981).

3. Lumsden and Wilson (1983), p. 171.

4. Konner (1982), p. 19.

5. The quotation is from Gould and Lewontin (1984), p. 264, as is the classification of three types of adaptation.

6. See, for example, Howard E. Gruber, "Genes for General Intellect Rather than for Particular Culture," *The Behavioral and Brain Sciences* 5: 11–12, 1982.

7. From the "Oration on the Dignity of Man" by Count Giovanni Pico della Mirandola, delivered in Rome in 1486.

8. The 99 percent overlap between human and chimp genomes refers to the entire nucleotide sequence contained in DNA. It has recently been established that only portions of the DNA molecule constitute the genetic message, while large sections are carried along, serving no known functions. They may be relics of prior events, or they may act as pools for further evolutionary changes. The genetically active portions of human and chimp DNA may thus differ by more than 1 percent. However, the recognition of the large noninformational portions of DNA further restrict the ability of the genome to provide detailed specification of brain structure. This was brought out at a recent meeting of neuroscientists; see Deborah M. Barnes, "Brain Architecture: Beyond Genes," *Science* 233: 155–156, 1986.

9. Gazzaniga and LeDoux (1978).

10. Konner (1982), p. 50.

11. The work by Thomas Wynn is reported by Roger Lewin, "Anthropologist Argues That Language Cannot Be Read in Stones," *Science* 233: 23–24, 1986.

12. The estimate on the size of the Neanderthal population in France is taken from Pfeiffer (1982).

13. The Neanderthal flower grave, known as Shanidar IV, is located in Iraq. It was reported by Ralph S. Solecki in 1975 and is described by Pfeiffer (1982), p. 99.

14. The description of the *cupule stone* at La Ferrassie is taken from Stern (1973), p. 30.

15. Kenneth M. Weiss, "On the Number of Members of the Genus *Homo* Who Have Ever Lived, and Some Evolutionary Implications," *Human Biology* 56: 637–649, 1984.

16. C. B. Stringer and P. Andrews, "Genetic and Fossil Evidence for the Origin of Modern Humans," *Science* 239: 1263–1268, 1988.

17. M. T. Smith and R. Layton, "Still Human after All These Years," *The Sciences* Jan/Feb 1989, p. 12.

18. This suggestion is from Stern (1973), p. 27.

19. Denis Vialou in a communication to Pfeiffer (1982), p. 141.

20. Pfeiffer (1982), p. 128.

21. The quotation by A. Leroi-Gourhan is from the introduction to Windels's (1949) photographic record of the cave paintings of Lascaux, p. 13.

22. Pfeiffer (1982), p. 180.

23. Ovid's *Metamorphoses*.

24. This story is reported by Allan C. Wilson, "The Molecular Basis of Evolution," *Scientific American*, October 1985, pp. 164–173.

CHAPTER IV

1. John Locke, English philosopher (1632–1704).

2. Good accounts of the roots of the eugenics movement and its subsequent spread are given by Morris (1983) and Kevles (1985). In this chapter I make liberal use of material presented and sources quoted by these two authors.

3. Morris (1983), p. 42.

4. The story of how Julian Schwinger, the famous American theoretical physicist, was admitted to Columbia University, is told by Jeremy Bernstein, "Personal History — The Life It Brings (Part I)," *The New Yorker*, January 26, 1987.

5. Kevles (1985), p. 97.

6. The story of Doris Buck is told by Gould in an epilogue to *The Mismeasure of Man* (1981), p. 335, which is dedicated to the debunking of the myth of the objectivity of the IQ test.

7. The extensive IQ tests carried out in the U.S. Army during World War I were reported by Yerkes (1921).

8. The quotation is from Stoddard (1923), who was one of the most outspoken and widely read commentators on the supposed superiority of the "Nordic race."

9. Wallace's quotation is taken from Kevles (1985), p. 70.

10. Stoddard (1923), p. 26.

11. R. Pearl's quotation is taken from Kevles (1985), p. 122.

12. O. Klineberg (1935), p. 155.

13. H. J. Eysenck's quotation is taken from Gould (1981), p. 235.

14. *Not in Our Genes*, by Lewontin, Rose, and Kamin, is a spirited, if at times tendentious, attack on genetic determinism and sociobiology (Lewontin et al., 1984), p. 24.

15. A discussion relevant to this point is given by Kevles (1985), p. 164. According to one estimate (*New York Times, Science Times*, April 21, 1987) every normal, healthy human carries about four detrimental genes.

16. This study by Stanford University psychiatrist Roy King was reported in *Time*, March 16, 1987.

17. Reference is to a paper by Arthur Jensen, "How Much Can We Boost IQ and Scholastic Achievement?" *Harvard Educational Review*, Winter 1969, pp. 1–123, which has been the object of considerable controversy.

18. In his review of Wilson and Herrnstein (1986), Jencks (1987) takes a position somewhat intermediate to the two viewpoints of pure genetic and environmental determinism (C. Jencks, Genes and Crime, *The New York Review of Books,* February 12, 1987).

19. The findings of James Flynn and similar results by other authors are discussed in a brief news report by Chris Brand entitled "Bryter Still and Bryter?" *Nature* (London) B 28: 110, 1987.

20. The quotation defining sociobiology is from Lumsden and Wilson (1983), p. 23. Some other important sources in the field of sociobiology are: Wilson (1975); Lumsden and Wilson (1981); Ruse (1979); Lewontin et al. (1984); Kitcher (1985); Sahlins (1976); Wilson (1978); Gould and Gould (1983); Lopreato (1984); Shapiro (1978).

21. The concept of "gene-culture coevolution" was introduced by Lumsden and Wilson (1981). See also the "Open Peer Commentary": Lumsden and Wilson, Précis of Genes, Mind, and Culture, *The Behavioral and Brain Sciences* 5: 1–37, 1982.

22. The quotation is from Lumsden and Wilson's article in *The Behavioral and Brain Sciences* (note 21), p. 21.

23. Gould and Lewontin (1984).

24. Gould (1981).

25. H. E. Gruber, "Genes for General Intellect Rather than for Particular Culture," *Behavior and Brain Science* 5: 11–12, 1982.

26. Dawkins (1976), pp. 49, 64.

27. Lewontin et al. (1984), p. 18.

CHAPTER V

1. Lewontin (1984), p. 68.

2. The quotation is from a review of B. F. Skinner's latest book (1987) by S. A. Barnett, "Rewards and Fairies," *Nature* (London) 382: 119, 1987.

3. Flanagan (1984), p. 268.

4. Strictly speaking, even the dynamics of planetary orbits become "intractable" if there is more than one planet in a solar system. In practice, we can calculate far enough into the future to consider the trajectories *predictable*.

5. The "butterfly effect" in meteorology was first discussed by E. N. Lorenz, "Deterministic Nonperiodic Flow," *Journal of the Atmospheric Sciences* 20: 130–141, 1963.

6. The term *strange attractors* refers to physical systems whose dynamics are attracted into a certain region. Unlike ordinary attractors, which cause repetitive behavior, like the movement of a clock pendulum, a system controlled by a strange attractor will behave differently in every cycle.

7. The quotations are from D. Ruelle, "Strange Attractors," *The Mathematical Intelligencer* 2: 126–137, 1980.

8. Cvitanovic (1984), p. 3. Our examples of the billiard table and the dice are complicated by the existence of unknown and unknowable external factors. They point up, however, the extreme sensitivity and consequent intracta-

bility of the problems. True "chaos" is said to exist in a physical system that is isolated, totally deterministic, but utterly unpredictable in the long run.

9. Gazzaniga (1985), p. 5.
10. Schroedinger (1944).
11. A discussion of self-transcendence appears in Harth (1982), p. 233.

CHAPTER VI

1. A number of good popular books on mind and brain have been published in recent years. The following is a partial and somewhat arbitrary list: Restak (1979); Brown (1977); Sagan (1977); Edelman and Mountcastle (1979); Harth (1982); Blakemore (1977); Edelman (1987); Searle (1984); Delbrueck (1985); Adam (1980).

2. The cerebrospinal fluid recently regained some of its earlier status, when it was realized that, apart from carrying away waste products, it also carries chemicals that have access to large portions of the brain through the walls of the ventricles. The role of these messengers in the processing of information is still being explored.

3. The point was made by the philosopher Adolf Gruenbaum (1984), in a critique of Freudian psychoanalysis.

4. Dyson's quotation is from an interview with Alvin P. Sanoff (*U.S. News & World Report,* April 18, 1988). See also Dyson's very readable book *Infinite in All Directions* (Dyson, 1988).

5. The so-called behaviorist school was founded by the American psychologist J. B. Watson, who made a radical break with earlier introspectionist views with his article "Psychology as the Behaviourist Views It," *Psychological Review* 20: 158–177, 1913.

6. Skinner (1987), p. 26.
7. Harth (1982).
8. Edelman (1987).
9. Oliver Sacks is known for his case history of mental diseases entitled *The Man Who Mistook His Wife for a Hat and Other Clinical Tales*. The story of Jonathan I. appeared in an article by O. Sacks and R. Wasserman, "The Case of the Colorblind Painter," *New York Review of Books,* November 19, 1987.

10. Bronowski (1973).
11. Gazzaniga (1985), p. 99.
12. The theory of perception referred to here was described in a number of technical papers by E. Harth and collaborators: "Visual Perception: A Dynamic Theory," *Biological Cybernetics* 22: 169–180 (1976); "Brainstem Control of Sensory Information," *International Journal of Psychophysiology* 3: 101–119 (1985); "The Inversion of Sensory Processes by Feedback Pathways," *Science* 237: 184–187 (1987). A brief nontechnical description appeared in my book (Harth, 1982).

13. Wiener's *circular causality* is described in H. von Foerster's book review entitled "Morality Play" of Steve J. Heims, *John von Neumann and Norbert Wiener: From Mathematics to the Technologies of Life and Death,* MIT Press, 1980. The review appeared in *The Sciences,* October 1981, pp. 24–25.

CHAPTER VII

1. A distinction between magic and religion is made, for example, by Malinowski (1948), who speaks of magic arts as acts performed for a definite purpose that is achieved later (spells, healing, etc.), whereas religious practices are generally ceremonial (rites of initiation, marriage). The existence of supernatural powers is, however, implied in both.

2. Donoghue (1983), p. 98.

3. Stone (1988), p. 70.

4. N. O. Brown's address to the Columbia University chapter of Phi Beta Kappa, the National Honor Society, entitled "Apocalypse: The Place of Mystery in the Life of the Mind," appeared in *Harper's,* May 1961.

5. Stone (1988), pp. 170–171.

6. Durant (1939), p. 522.

7. The point that astrology began as a science linking the apparent chaos of earth to celestial rules was recently made by S. J. Tester (1987). He makes the point also that astrology did not originate in Egypt or Babylonia, as is often claimed, but is a product of Western, that is, Greek, thought.

8. A report on the study by People for the American Way appeared in the *New York Times, Science Times,* September 16, 1986.

9. Paracelsus was one of the most colorful figures of early sixteenth-century Europe. The two passages quoted here are from a newly translated and edited edition of his works by Arthur Edward Waite (1976), vol. 2, p. 5.

10. From the prologue to the *Archidoxies* by Paracelsus. Waite (1976), vol. 2, p. 9.

11. Poincaré (1952).

12. This quotation from Xenophon's *Memorabilia* is taken from Sarton (1952), p. 260.

13. Early in 1989 two chemists caused a flurry of excitement when they announced that they had produced energy from controlled nuclear fusion in a particularly simple experiment. The hopes for a quick and clean solution to the world's energy problems quickly faded, however, when subsequent research by other scientists failed to confirm these results.

14. See note 4.

15. See note 2.

16. Hawking (1988), p. 155.

17. Physicists recognize four fundamental forces, or interactions, in nature: the *gravitational* interaction, which is the weakest, the so-called *weak* interaction that is responsible for radioactive decay, the *electromagnetic* interaction, which accounts for most of the chemical properties of matter, and the *nuclear force,* which is by far the strongest of the four and holds together the nuclei of atoms. A fifth, and even a sixth force have been claimed but have not been confirmed. Much of contemporary theoretical physics is concerned with arriving at a unified picture of these interactions. A discussion of unification attempts can be found in Hawking (1988), p. 155.

18. The quotation is from S. Glashow, "Tangled in Superstring: Some Thoughts on the Predicament Physics Is In," *The Sciences,* May/June 1988, pp. 22–25.

19. K. C. Cole, "A Theory of Everything," *New York Times Magazine*, October 18, 1987.

20. Scientists now talk about events 10^{-36} seconds (one billionth of a billionth of a billionth of a billionth of a second) after the big bang. This earliest portion of the evolution of the universe is described in a semipopular article by D. N. Schramm and G. Steigman, "Particle Accelerators Test Cosmological Theory," *Scientific American*, June 1988.

21. Capra, *The Tao of Physics* (1975).

22. Hawking's expression quoted here is from an article in the *New York Times*, *Science Times* (April 19, 1988) by Malcolm W. Browne, entitled "Mystics and Science: Hawking's Views."

23. See the article by Philip M. Boffey: "Two Leaders Challenge the 'Big Science' Trend," *New York Times*, *Science Times*, May 3, 1988.

24. Heinz von Foerster used that expression in his article "Morality Play" (see note 13, chapter VI) reviewing Heims (1980), in which the author examines the question "how it happens that honorable and sophisticated men knowingly engage in actions likely eventually to give rise to destruction and misery. . . ."

CHAPTER VIII

1. Orwell (1961), p. 246.

2. The classic *Principles of Psychology* by William James was republished by Dover Press in 1950. The quotation is from vol. 1, p. 54.

3. Philip Lieberman, "Voice in the Wilderness," *The Sciences*, July/August, 1988.

4. The quotation is from Octavio Paz's essay "Literature and Literalness in Convergences" (Paz, 1987).

5. Chase (1938).

6. Sampson (1802), p. 52.

7. Chase (1938), p. 5.

8. Chase (1938), p. 81.

9. Donoghue (1983), p. 117.

10. From *The New Yorker*, "Talk of the Town," June 27, 1988.

11. William Safire, "On Language," *New York Times Magazine*, December 14, 1986.

12. Tom Wicker in the *New York Times*, October 19, 1986.

CHAPTER IX

1. Lester Brown has written a series of books dedicated to a study of the most pressing global problems confronting us in the coming decades. Brown (1974, 1984, 1985, 1988).

2. The *doomsday equation* was published in an article by Heinz von Foerster, Patricia M. Mora, and Lawrence W. Amiot, "Doomsday: Friday, 13 November, A.D. 2026," *Science* 132: 1291–1295, 1960.

3. The data on the effects of an attack on the American nuclear deterrent forces are taken from Frank N. von Hippel, Barbara G. Levi, Theodore A.

Postol, and William H. Dougherty, "Civilian Casualties from Counterforce Attacks," *Scientific American,* September 1988, pp. 36–42.

4. De Loyola Brandão (1985).

5. Some of the data on the greenhouse effect are taken from V. Ramanathan's "The Greenhouse Theory of Climate Changes: A Test by an Inadvertent Global Experiment," *Science* 240: 293–299, 1988.

6. R. Buddemeier, quoted by A. C. Revkin, "Living with the Greenhouse Effect," *Discover,* October 1988, pp. 50–61.

7. V. A. Mohnen, "The Challenge of Acid Rain," *Scientific American,* August 1988.

8. Data on the projected nuclear storage site in Yucca Mountain are taken from R. Monastersky, "The 10,000-Year Test," *Science News,* February 27, 1988.

9. Such awards were in fact instituted in 1980 by Jakob von Uexkull, a member of the European Parliament. They are called the Right Livelihood awards and are intended for "those working on practicable and replicable solutions to the real problems facing us today."

CHAPTER X

1. Brodsky (1986), p. 3.

2. B. Bower, "Murder in Good Company," *Science News* 133: 90–91, 1988.

3. N. A. Chagnon, "Life Histories, Blood Revenge, and Warfare in a Tribal Population," *Science* 239: 985–992, 1988.

4. Lee Smolin, "Space and Time in the Quantum Universe," *Proceedings of the Osgood Hill Conference on Quantum Gravity,* A. Ashtekar and J. Stachel (eds.), 1989, in press.

5. Brodsky (1986), p. 65.

6. Millennial movements in the United States in the nineteenth century and their connection with present trends are discussed in two books by Barkun (1974, 1986).

Selected Bibliography

Ádám, G. (1980). *Perception, Consciousness, Memory*. New York: Plenum Press.

Barkun, Michael (1974). *Disaster and the Millennium*. New Haven: Yale University Press.

Barkun, Michael (1986). *Crucible of the Millennium*. Syracuse: Syracuse University Press.

Blakemore, Colin (1977). *Mechanism of the Mind*. Cambridge: Cambridge University Press.

Brandão, Ignacio de Loyola (1982). *And Still the Earth*. English trans., New York: Avon Books, 1985.

Brodsky, Joseph (1986). *Less Than One*. New York: Farrar Straus and Giroux.

Bronowski, Jacob (1973). *The Ascent of Man*. Boston: Little, Brown.

Brown, Jason W. (1977). *Mind, Brain and Consciousness*. New York: Academic Press.

Brown, Lester R. (1974). *In the Human Interest: A Strategy to Stabilize World Population*. New York: W. W. Norton.

Brown, Lester R. (1984). *Soil Erosion: Quiet Crisis in the World Economy*. Washington, D.C.: Worldwatch Institute.

Brown, Lester R. (1985). *State of the World 1985: A Worldwatch Institute Report on Progress Toward a Sustainable Society*. New York: W. W. Norton.

Brown, Lester R. (1988). *The Changing World Food Prospect: The Nineties and Beyond*. Washington, D.C.: Worldwatch Institute.

Capra, Fritjof (1975). *The Tao of Physics*. Boulder, Colo.: Shambala.

Chase, Stuart (1938). *The Tyranny of Words*. New York: Harcourt Brace.

Cvitanovic, Predrag (ed.) (1984). *Universality in Chaos*. Bristol, England: Adam Hilger Ltd.

Dawkins, Richard (1976). *The Selfish Gene*. New York: Oxford University Press.

Cohn, Norman (1961). *The Pursuit of the Millennium*. New York: Harper.

Daniel, Norman (1975). *The Arabs and Medieval Europe*. London: Longman.

Delbrück, Max (1985). *Mind from Matter*. Boston: Blackwell.

Donoghue, Denis (1983). *The Arts without Mystery*. Boston: Little, Brown.

Durant, Will (1939). *The Life of Greece*. New York: Simon and Schuster.

Durant, Will (1950). *The Age of Faith*. New York: Simon and Schuster.

Dyson, Freeman (1988). *Infinite in All Directions*. New York: Harper and Row.

Edelman, Gerald M. (1987). *Neural Darwinism: The Theory of Neuronal Group Selection*. New York: Basic Books.

Edelman, G. M., and V. B. Mountcastle (1979). *The Mindful Brain*. Cambridge, Mass.: MIT Press.

Eldredge, Niles, and Stephen J. Gould (1972). "Punctuated Equilibria: An

Alternative to Phyletic Gradualism," in *Models of Paleobiology*, T. J. M. Schopf and J. M. Thomas (eds.). San Francisco: Freeman Cooper.

Flanagan, Owen J. (1984). *The Science of the Mind*. Cambridge, Mass.: MIT Press.

Galton, Francis (1869). *Hereditary Genius: An Inquiry into Its Laws and Consequences*. London: Macmillan.

Gazzaniga, Michael S. (1985). *The Social Brain: Discovering the Networks of the Mind*. New York: Basic Books.

Gazzaniga, Michael S., and J. E. LeDoux (1978). *The Integrated Brain*. New York: Plenum Press.

Goodall, Jane (1986). *The Chimpanzees of Gombe*. Cambridge, Mass.: Belknap Press of Harvard University Press.

Gould, Stephen J. (1981). *The Mismeasure of Man*. New York: W. W. Norton.

Gould, J. L., and C. Gould (1983). "Advanced Sociobiology." *Harper's*, June.

Gould, Stephen J., and Richard C. Lewontin (1984). "The Spandrels of San Marco and the Panglossian Paradigm: A Critique of the Adaptionist Programme," in *Conceptual Issues in Evolutionary Biology*, E. Sober (ed.). Cambridge, Mass.: MIT Press.

Gruenbaum, Adolf (1984). *The Foundations of Psychoanalysis: A Philosophical Critique*. Berkeley, Calif.: University of California Press.

Harth, Erich (1982). *Windows on the Mind*. New York: Morrow.

Hawking, Stephen W. (1988). *A Brief History of Time: From Big Bang to Black Holes*. New York: Bantam.

Heims, Steve J. (1980). *John von Neumann and Norbert Wiener: From Mathematics to the Technologies of Life and Death*. Cambridge, Mass.: MIT Press.

James, William (1950). *The Principles of Psychology*. New York: Dover.

Kaufmann, Walter (ed. and transl.) (1954). *The Portable Nietzsche*. New York: Viking Press.

Kevles, Daniel J. (1985). *In the Name of Eugenics*. Berkeley, Calif.: University of California Press.

Kitcher, Philip (1985). *Vaulting Ambition: Sociobiology and the Quest for Human Nature*. Cambridge, Mass.: MIT Press.

Klineberg, Otto (1935). *Race Differences*. New York: Harper and Row.

Konner, Melvin (1982). *The Tangled Wing: Biological Constraints on the Human Spirit*. New York: Holt, Rinehart and Winston.

Lewontin, Richard C. (1984). "The Structure of Evolutionary Genetics," in *Conceptual Issues in Evolutionary Biology*, E. Sober (ed.). Cambridge, Mass.: MIT Press.

Lewontin, Richard C., S. Rose, and Leon J. Kamin (1984). *Not in Our Genes*. New York: Pantheon.

Locke, John (1690). *An Essay Concerning Human Understanding*. Oxford: Clarendon Press, 1975.

Lopez, Roberto S. (1964). *The Tenth Century*. New York: Holt, Rinehart and Winston.

Lopreato, Joseph (1984). *Human Nature and Biocultural Evolution*. Boston: Allen and Unwin.

Lumsden, Charles J., and Edwin O. Wilson (1981). *Genes, Mind, and Culture.* Cambridge, Mass.: Harvard University Press.
Lumsden, Charles J., and Edwin O. Wilson (1983). *Promethean Fire: Reflections on the Origin of Mind.* Cambridge, Mass.: Harvard University Press.
Malinowski, Bronislaw (1948). *Magic, Science and Religion.* New York: Doubleday.
Marshak, Alexander (1972). *The Roots of Civilization.* New York: McGraw-Hill.
Mayr, Ernst (1982). *The Growth of Biological Thought.* Cambridge, Mass.: Belknap Press of Harvard University Press.
Mayr, Ernst (1984). "Typological Versus Population Thinking," in *Conceptual Issues in Evolutionary Biology,* E. Sober (ed.). Cambridge, Mass.: MIT Press.
Mojtabai, Grace (1986). *Blessed Assurance: At Home with the Bomb in Amarillo, Texas.* Boston: Houghton Mifflin.
Morris, Richard (1983). *Evolution and Human Nature.* New York: Putnam.
Orwell, George (1961). *1984.* New York: New American Library.
Paz, Octavio (1987). *Convergences: Essays on Art and Literature.* New York: Harcourt Brace Jovanovich.
Pfeiffer, John E. (1982). *The Creative Explosion.* New York: Harper and Row.
Pico della Mirandola, Giovanni (1486). *Oration on the Dignity of Man,* A. R. Caponigri, transl. Chicago: Gateway Editions, Inc., 1956.
Poincaré, Henri (1952). *Science and Hypothesis.* New York: Dover.
Provine, William B. (1986). *Sewall Wright and Evolutionary Biology.* Chicago: University of Chicago Press.
Restak, Richard (1979). *The Brain: The Last Frontier.* New York: Doubleday.
Ruse, Michael (1979). *Sociobiology: Sense or Nonsense?* Boston: Reidel.
Sacks, Oliver (1985). *The Man Who Mistook His Wife for a Hat and Other Clinical Tales.* New York: Summit Books.
Sagan, Carl (1977). *The Dragons of Eden.* New York: Random House.
Sahlins, Marshall D. (1976). *The Use and Abuse of Biology: An Anthropological Critique of Sociobiology.* Ann Arbor, Mich.: University of Michigan Press.
Sampson, Ezra (1802). *The Sham Patriot Unmasked, or An Exposition of the Fatally Successful Arts of Demagogues.* Middletown, Conn.: T. and J. B. Dunning.
Sarton, George (1952). *A History of Science.* Cambridge, Mass.: Harvard University Press.
Schroedinger, Erwin (1944). *What is Life? and Mind and Matter.* New York: Cambridge University Press.
Searle, John (1984). *Minds, Brains and Science.* Cambridge, Mass.: Harvard University Press.
Shapiro, Mark (1978). *The Sociobiology of Homo Sapiens.* Kansas City, Mo.: The Pinecrest Fund.
Silberbauer, George (1981). "Hunter/Gatherer of the Kalahari," in *Omnivorous Primates,* R. Harding and G. Teleki (eds.). New York: Columbia University Press.

Skinner, B. F. (1987). *Upon Further Reflection*. Englewood Cliffs, N.J.: Prentice Hall.

Stern, Philip Van Doren (1973). *The Beginnings of Art*. New York: Four Winds Press.

Stoddard, Theodore L. (1923). *The Revolt against Civilization: The Menace of the Under Man*. New York: Charles Scribner's Sons.

Stone, I. F. (1988). *The Trial of Socrates*. Boston: Little, Brown.

Tester, S. Jim (1987). *A History of Western Astrology*. Wolfeboro, N.H.: Boydell and Brewer.

Waite, A. E. (ed.) (1976). *The Hermetic and Alchemical Writings of Aureolus Philippus Theophrastus Bombast of Hohenheim, called Paracelsus the Great*. Berkeley, Calif.: Shambala.

Washburn, Sherwood L., and R. Moore (1977). *Ape into Human*. Boston: Little, Brown.

Wendt, Herbert (1972). *From Ape to Adam*. Indianapolis, Ind.: Bobbs Merrill.

Wilson, Edward O. (1975). *Sociobiology: The New Synthesis*. Cambridge, Mass.: Belknap Press of Harvard University Press.

Wilson, Edward O. (1978). *On Human Nature*. Cambridge, Mass.: Harvard University Press.

Wilson, James Q., and Richard J. Herrnstein (1986). *Crime and Human Nature*. New York: Simon and Schuster.

Windels, Fernand (1949). *The Lascaux Cave Paintings*. London: Faber and Faber.

Yerkes, R. M. (ed.) (1921). "Psychological Examining in the US Army." *Memoirs of National Academy of Science*, vol. 15.

Index